Multiple Choice Q

Principles of Accounts

Second Edition

E. R. Martin FCCA

Edward Arnold
A division of Hodder & Stoughton
LONDON BALTIMORE MELBOURNE AUCKLAND

Acknowledgements

The author wishes to thank the staff of the Commerce Department of the Barry College of Further Education for their advice, encouragement and assistance.

First published in Great Britain 1980
Third impression 1988
Second edition 1988

British Library Cataloguing in Publication Data

Martin, E.R. (Ernest Richard), *1915–*
Multiple choice questions on the principles of accounts.—2nd ed.
1. Accounting, Questions & answers
I. Title
657′076

ISBN 0–7131–7748–9

Typeset in 10/11pt Times by Colset Pte. Ltd., Singapore
Printed and bound in Great Britain for Edward Arnold, the educational, academic and medical publishing division of Hodder and Stoughton Limited, 41 Bedford Square, London WC1B 3DQ by Richard Clay plc, Bungay, Suffolk

Contents

Preface

This book, which has been thoroughly revised and updated for the second edition, contains over 400 multiple choice questions on accounting topics at GCSE level. It will also be useful for students following LCCI, RSA, BTEC First and National, and foundation professional courses.

The questions have been arranged in two sections. Section 1 contains 19 chapters, the first 16 of which deal with specific topics, while chapters 17, 18 and 19 contain questions on a variety of topics graded 'easy', 'harder' and 'difficult'. In this section the student is required to select one correct answer. In Section 2, which has been added for this new edition, there may be one or more correct solution to the questions and the student is required to make a choice using the code given at the beginning of the section.

The book will assist students in their revision by testing the effectiveness of their study. Some of the questions may also be used as the basis for assignment work. Answers to the questions are given at the back of the book.

SECTION 1

In this section you are required to select the most appropriate answer to the question or incomplete statement.

1

Books of prime entry and the ledger

1 A debit balance of £60 on a Cash Account means that
- **A** the total money received was £60
- **B** the total money paid out was £60
- **C** there is £60 cash in hand
- **D** there is £60 in the bank

2 The total of the Purchases Day Book is posted to the
- **A** debit of the Purchases Account
- **B** credit of the Purchases Account
- **C** credit of the personal accounts of the firms from whom the goods were bought
- **D** credit of the Sales Account

3 The total of the Sales Day Book is posted to the
- **A** debit of the Sales Account
- **B** credit of the Sales Account
- **C** debit of the personal accounts of the firms to whom goods were sold
- **D** credit of the Purchases Account

4 The total of the Purchases Returns Day Book is posted to the
- **A** credit of the Returns Outwards Account
- **B** debit of the Returns Outwards Account
- **C** credit of the Returns Inwards Account
- **D** debit of the Returns Inwards Account

5 Invoices received for goods purchased should first be entered in the
- **A** Sales Day Book
- **B** Purchases Account
- **C** Purchases Day Book
- **D** Cash Book

6 A credit note received from a supplier should first be entered in the
A Purchases Returns Day Book
B Sales Returns Day Book
C Returns Inwards Account
D Returns Outwards Account

7 C. Charles, an estate agent, purchased a car on credit for use in his business. This transaction should first be entered in the
A Cash Book
B Journal Proper
C Ledger
D Purchases Day Book

8 Cash discounts received when paying an account should be shown in
A the Cash Book and Suppliers' Account only
B Discount Account and the Suppliers' Account only
C Discount Account, the Suppliers' Account and the Cash Book
D none of the above

9 The total of the discounts received column in the Cash Book is posted to the
A debit of the Discounts Received Account
B debit of the Discounts Allowed Account
C credit of the Discounts Received Account
D credit of the Discounts Allowed Account

10 Cash discount is given
A only when goods are bought for cash
B when accounts are paid according to the terms of payment
C when dealing with other traders only
D only when goods are paid for by cash or cheque

11 Trade discount is shown in the
A Sales or Purchases Day Books only
B Sales or Purchases Day Books and the Ledger
C Cash Book only
D Cash Book and the Ledger

12 An invoice dated 20 March shows a total of £120 less 33.33% trade discount and 5% cash discount if paid by the 10th of the following month. If the account is paid on 5 April, the cheque will be for
A £120 **B** £76 **C** £74 **D** £80

13 Which of the following accounts is a Personal Account?
A Van Account
B Wages Account
C Sundry Expenses Account
D The Cardiff Wholesalers Ltd's Account

14 Which of the following accounts is a Real Account?
A Capital Account
B Fixtures and Fittings Account
C Sundry Expenses Account
D Discounts Received Account

15 Which of the following is a Nominal Account?
- **A** Wages Account
- **B** Motor Van Account
- **C** Capital Account
- **D** J. Samuel & Sons' Account

16 A balance in the Petty Cash Book is
- **A** shown as sundry expenses in the Profit and Loss Account
- **B** not shown as it is included in the Sundry Expenses Account
- **C** deducted from the balance of the Cash Account
- **D** shown in the Balance Sheet as cash in hand

17 Impersonal Accounts are those that
- **A** relate to debtors
- **B** relate to capital
- **C** comprise both Real and Nominal Accounts
- **D** relate to creditors

18 Real Accounts are those that
- **A** refer to property and material objects
- **B** have debit entries only
- **C** refer to liabilities
- **D** relate to gains and losses

19 Credit balances on accounts are
- **A** either liabilities or gains
- **B** either assets or losses
- **C** profits only
- **D** losses only

20 Debit balances on accounts are
- **A** assets, expenses or losses
- **B** liabilities or gains
- **C** profits only
- **D** losses only

2
Principles of double entry

1 The balances shown in the Trial Balance are taken from the Ledger
- **A** on the same side
- **B** on the opposite side
- **C** and the Day Books on the same side
- **D** and the Day Books on the opposite side

2 The double entry for a purchase from C. Charles and Sons entered in the Purchases Day Book and posted to C. Charles and Sons' Account is to be found
- **A** in the Purchases Day Book
- **B** in the Purchases Account
- **C** in the Cash or Bank Account
- **D** in the Goods Received Account

3 A debit balance of £122 on P. Evans Ltd's Account in the books of R. Rowlands means that
- **A** P. Evans Ltd owes R. Rowlands £122
- **B** R. Rowlands owes P. Evans Ltd £122
- **C** P. Evans Ltd has paid R. Rowlands £122
- **D** R. Rowlands has paid P. Evans Ltd £122

4 If a sales return of £20 had been posted wrongly to the credit of the Returns Outwards Account, the totals of the Trial Balance will show the credit side to be
- **A** £20 more than the debit side
- **B** £20 less than the debit side
- **C** £40 more than the debit side
- **D** £40 less than the debit side

5 Mr A. Jones introduces a further £1000 cash into his business. The necessary entries to record this transaction in the Ledger will be
- **A** debit Cash Account, credit Sales Account
- **B** debit Capital Account, credit Cash Account
- **C** debit Cash Account only
- **D** debit Cash Account, credit Capital Account

6 The proprietor of a business withdraws cash for his own use. The necessary entries in the Ledger to record this transaction will be
- **A** debit Cash Account, credit Bank Account
- **B** debit Cash Account, credit Drawings Account
- **C** debit Drawings Account, credit Cash Account
- **D** debit Bank Account, credit Cash Account

7 S. Paul, who owns a menswear shop, makes the following payments. Which of these is considered to be capital expenditure?

A Purchase of 12 raincoats
B Payment of £200 for wages
C Purchase of a van
D Payment £6 for sundry expenses

8 The owner of a business takes stock for his own use. The entries necessary to record this are

A debit Cash Account, credit Drawings Account
B debit Drawings Account, credit Sales Account
C debit Capital Account, credit Drawings Account
D debit Stock Account, credit Drawings Account

9 A Bank Overdraft is shown as a

A credit balance on an Overdraft Account
B debit balance on an Overdraft Account
C credit balance on the Bank Account
D debit balance on the Bank Account

10 A company receives a loan of £3000 from A. Paul. The entries necessary to record this transaction are

A debit Bank Account, credit Loan Account
B debit Loan Account, credit Bank Account
C debit Cash Account only
D debit Cash Account, credit Capital Account

11 The entries necessary to record the payment of interest on a loan are

A debit Bank Account, credit Loan Account
B debit Loan Account, credit Bank Account
C debit Loan Interest Account, credit Bank Account
D debit Bank Account, credit Loan Interest Account

12 The entries necessary to record interest received are

A debit Bank Account, credit Loan Account
B debit Loan Account, credit Bank Account
C debit Bank Account, credit Loan Interest Received Account
D debit Loan Interest Received Account, credit Bank Account

13 If a cheque for £95, received in settlement of an account for £100 from which a cash discount of £5 had been deducted, was returned by the bank marked R/D, then the entries for this transaction will be

A debit Personal Account £90, credit Bank Account £90
B debit Discount Account £5, credit Bank Account £95
C debit Personal Account £100, credit Bank Account £95 and Discount Account £5
D debit Personal Account £95 and Discount Account £5, credit Bank Account £100

14 When petty cash is kept on the imprest system then
A a fixed amount is drawn from the cashier every week
B the petty cashier is reimbursed every week with the total expenditure for the week
C there is no need for analysis columns in the Petty Cash Book
D the balance at the end of every week is the total expenditure for that week

******

Consider the following Loan Account in the books of S. Smith and then answer questions 15–18.

A. Adams (Loan Account)

19—			£		19—			£	
31 Dec	Bank		1200	00	1 Jan	Bank		4000	00
31 Dec	Balance	c/d	3200	00	31 Dec	Interest		400	00
			4400	00				4400	00
19–1					19–1				
31 Dec	Bank		1200	00	1 Jan	Balance	b/d	3200	00
31 Dec	Balance	c/d	2320	00	31 Dec	Interest		320	00
			3520	00				3520	00
					19–2				
					1 Jan	Balance	b/d	2320	00

15 The money is borrowed
A by A. Adams
B by S. Smith
C from the bank
D from S. Smith

16 What rate of interest has been charged?
A 5% per annum on the total amount borrowed
B 5% per annum on the balance at 1 January every year
C 5% every half year
D 10% per annum on the balance outstanding at 1 January every year

17 How much was on loan on 1 January 19–1?
A £4000 **B** £3200 **C** £3520 **D** none of these

18 Assume the rate of interest to be the same and nothing further has been repaid, how much would be needed to pay off the loan on 31 December 19–2?
A £2000 **B** £2552 **C** £3520 **D** £2400

19 D. Perkins' Account in a firm's ledger shows a debit balance of £200 on 1 January 19—. During the month of January the firm sold goods to D. Perkins invoiced at £250 less 20% trade discount, and received a cheque from D. Perkins for £156 on account after a cash discount of $2\frac{1}{2}$% had been deducted. The balance on the account on 31 January 19— will be

A £240 debit **B** £224 debit **C** £290 debit **D** £290 credit

20 A. Sharp, a newsagent, purchased a new van for £7500 on credit from South Wales Motors Ltd, who took his old van valued in the books at £500 in part exchange, allowing him £350 for it. The entries to record this transaction in the ledger will be

A debit Van Account £7500 and South Wales Motors Ltd Account £350, credit South Wales Motors Ltd Account £7500 and Van Account £350

B debit Van Account £7500 and South Wales Motors Ltd Account £350 and Loss on Sale of Van Account £150, credit South Wales Motors Ltd Account £7500 and Van Account £500

C debit Van Account £7500 and South Wales Motors Ltd Account £350 and Loss on Sale of Van Account £150, credit South Wales Motors Ltd Account £7150 and Van Account £500

D debit Van Account £7500 and Van Account £350 and Loss on Sale of Van Account £150, credit South Wales Motors Ltd Account £7500 and South Wales Motors Ltd Account £500

3

Provisions and adjustments

1 Rent paid in advance is shown as
A a debit balance on the Rent Account
B a credit balance on the Rent Account
C a liability in the Balance Sheet
D a debit in the Trading Account

2 Wages accrued are shown as
A a debit balance on the Wages Account
B a credit balance on the Wages Account
C a fixed asset in the Balance Sheet
D a current asset in the Balance Sheet

3 The amount shown in the Profit and Loss Account as rent should be
A the total amount paid for rent during the period
B the actual amount that should have been paid during the period
C the actual payments for rent plus any amounts due
D the actual amounts paid for rent plus any premium for the lease

4 Premises were let on 1 January 19–1 at an annual rental of £5000 and the amounts paid for rent during the year ended 30 June 19–1 totalled £3750. The rent to be shown in the Profit and Loss Account for the year ended 30 June 19–1 should be
A £3750 **B** £2500 **C** £5000 **D** £625

******

Consider the following Rent Account and then answer questions 5–7.

Rent Account

19–1			£		19–1			£	
1 Jan	Balance	b/d	250	00					
10 Jan	Bank		500	00					
5 Apr	Bank		500	00					
12 Jul	Bank		500	00	31 Dec	Transfer			
15 Oct	Bank		500	00		P&L Account		2000	00
28 Dec	Bank		500	00	31 Dec	Balance	c/d	750	00
			2750	00				2750	00
19–2									
1 Jan	Balance	b/d	750	00					

5 The balance of £750 represents
- **A** rent paid in advance
- **B** rent due
- **C** rent accrued
- **D** an increase in rent

6 The annual rental is
A £2750 **B** £250 **C** £2500 **D** £2000

7 If the rent is increased to £4000 per annum as from 1 January 19–2 then the rent due on 31 March 19–2 will be
A £750 **B** £1000 **C** £250 **D** £1750

8 A Trial Balance showed rent £600 on the credit. This means
- **A** £600 was paid for rent during the period
- **B** £600 included the amounts paid plus any amount paid in advance last year
- **C** £600 was the amount paid less any amount paid in advance this year
- **D** that the Rent Receivable Account showed a credit balance of £600

9 A Trial Balance showed wages £12 500 and a note stated that £500 wages were due but unpaid. When preparing final accounts the entries should be
- **A** debit Profit and Loss Account £13 000 and show Wages Accrued £500 in the Balance Sheet
- **B** debit Profit and Loss Account £12 000 and show Wages Accrued £500 in the Balance Sheet
- **C** debit Profit and Loss Account £13 000 and show Wages Prepaid £500 in the Balance Sheet
- **D** debit Profit and Loss Account £11 500 and show Wages Paid in Advance £500 in the Balance Sheet

******

Consider the following combined Rent and Rates Account and then answer questions 10–16.

Rent and Rates Account

19—			£		19—			£	
1 Jan	Balance (rates)	b/d	280	00					
20 Mar	Bank (rent)		400	00					
4 May	Bank (rates)		560	00	31 Dec	Transfer			
14 Jul	Bank (rent)		400	00		P&L A/C		2760	00
26 Nov	Bank (rent)		400	00	31 Dec	Balance			
30 Nov	Bank (rates)		640	00		(rates)	c/d	320	00
31 Dec	Balance (rent)		400	00					
			3080	00				3080	00
19–1					19–1				
1 Jan	Balance (rates)	b/d	320	00	1 Jan	Balance			
						(rent)	b/d	400	00

10 The annual rental is
A £1200 **B** £1400 **C** £1600 **D** £1800

11 The annual rates are
A £1120 **B** £1160 **C** £1200 **D** £1480

12 The Balance £280 on 1 January 19— represents
A rates accrued as at 1 January 19—
B rates paid in advance as at 1 January 19—
C rates refunded during the year
D none of the above

13 The credit balance of £400 is
A rent paid in advance
B rates paid in advance
C rent accrued
D rent prepaid

14 The rates paid in advance are
A £320 **B** £400 **C** £280 **D** nil

15 The total amount of rent paid during the year was
A £1200 **B** £1480 **C** £1600 **D** £1800

16 The total amount of rates paid during the year was
A £1200 **B** £1120 **C** £1480 **D** £880

17 The Profit and Loss Account showed rent payable £1500 and the Balance Sheet showed rent paid in advance £500. The actual amount paid for rent during the year
A was £1500
B was £1000
C was £2000
D cannot be calculated from the information given

18 A company sub-let part of its premises from 1 April 19— at an annual rental of £1000 of which £500 was received on 1 May and £500 on 1 November. The company prepares its accounts to 31 December. The entry for rent in the Profit and Loss Account for the year ended 31 December 19— should be
A £750 debit **B** £750 credit **C** £1000 debit **D** £1000 credit

19 The Balance Sheet as at year ended 31 December 19—, of the company in question 18 should show
A rent due £250 as a current asset
B rent received in advance £250 as a current liability
C no item for rent due or rent paid in advance
D rent receivable £1000 as a current asset

20 One of the main problems when preparing Final Accounts is to
A obtain exact figures of sales and purchases
B get the books up to date
C decide what revenue and expenses are attributable to that period
D decide which items should be in the Trading Account, the Profit and Loss Account or the Balance Sheet

4

Trading and profit and loss accounts

1 Gross profit is
   A sales minus purchases
   B net profit minus expenses
   C sales minus cost of goods sold
   D sales minus purchases plus stock at start

2 The cost of goods sold is the same as
   A purchases
   B sales
   C sales minus cost of sales
   D stock at start plus purchases minus stock at end

3 If stock at start is £1420, stock at end £1590, purchases £15 600, sales £17 800. The cost of sales is
   A £12 100 **B** £15 430 **C** £17 800 **D** £15 600

4 If stock at start is £1510, stock at end £1640, sales £24 610, purchases £13 060. The gross profit is
   A £11 550 **B** £1910 **C** £11 420 **D** £11 680

5 If gross profit is £620 and sales £2480, then the percentage gross profit to sales is
   A 40% **B** 50% **C** 25% **D** $33\frac{1}{3}$%

6 If percentage gross profit to sales is 25% and sales are £8600 the gross profit is
   A £2400 **B** £2150 **C** £2000 **D** £4300

7 If the percentage of gross profit to cost of sales is 25% and sales are £9000, the gross profit
   A will be £2250
   B will be £3000
   C will be £1800
   D cannot be calculated from the information given

8 Net profit is
   A the increase in cash
   B sales less all expenditure including purchases
   C sales less all expenditure other than purchases
   D gross profit less expenses

9 If the gross profit is £16 920 and the following payments have been made: rent £300, rates £280, wages £4600, furniture and fittings £1320, then the net profit will be
   A £10 420 **B** £11 400 **C** £12 320 **D** £11 740

10 The value of the stock shown in the Trading Account is usually found by
A deducting the purchases from the sales
B counting the stock and then valuing it at cost price
C counting the stock and then valuing it at selling price
D using a fixed percentage of sales

11 Which of the following items does *not* appear in the Profit and Loss Account?
A Discounts **B** Wages **C** Furniture and fittings **D** Rents receivable

12 If the stock at start were undervalued then the
A gross profit will be overstated
B gross profit will be understated
C gross profit will be unaffected
D net profit will be understated

13 If the stock at the end were undervalued then the
A gross profit will be overstated
B gross profit will be understated
C gross profit will be unaffected
D net profit will be overstated

14 The double entry for the net profit is found
A in the Bank Account
B on the debit of the Capital Account
C on the credit of the Capital Account
D in the Balance Sheet

15 The cash discounts received are shown
A on the debit of Profit and Loss Account
B on the credit of Profit and Loss Account
C in the Trading Account
D in the Balance Sheet

16 Carriage inwards is shown on the
A debit of Profit and Loss Account
B credit of Profit and Loss Account
C debit of Trading Account
D credit of Trading Account

17 Carriage outwards is shown on the
A debit of Profit and Loss Account
B credit of Profit and Loss Account
C debit of Trading Account
D credit of Trading Account

18 When sales increase
A gross profit must increase
B net profit must increase
C both net and gross profit must increase
D it does not necessarily follow that the profits will increase

19 Commission and rent may appear on
- **A** debit side of Profit and Loss Account only
- **B** credit side of Profit and Loss Account only
- **C** either side of Profit and Loss Account
- **D** either side of Trading Account

20 A trader's mark-up of 25% means a gross profit of
- **A** 25% on invoice price
- **B** 25% on selling price
- **C** 20% on cost of sales
- **D** $33\frac{1}{3}$% on selling price

5
Balance sheets

1 A Balance Sheet is
- **A** part of the double entry
- **B** a Ledger Account
- **C** a statement of outstanding balances after the preparation of the Trading and Profit and Loss Account
- **D** prepared only to prove the arithmetic accuracy of the accounts

2 Which of the following items of information could not be obtained from the Balance Sheet?
- **A** Value of the assets
- **B** Extent of the liabilities
- **C** Gross profit
- **D** Whether the business is solvent or not

3 Which of the following is an asset?
- **A** Creditors
- **B** Bank Overdraft
- **C** Premises
- **D** Capital

4 Which of the following is a liability?
- **A** Debtors
- **B** Bank overdraft
- **C** Rates paid in advance
- **D** A loan to a director of a company

5 After preparing a Balance Sheet a cheque for £40 was paid to a creditor. The alterations to the Balance Sheet will be
- **A** an increase of £40 in the Debtors Account and a decrease of £40 in the Creditors Account
- **B** a decrease of £40 in the cash at bank only
- **C** a decrease of £40 in the cash at bank and a decrease of £40 in Creditors Account
- **D** a decrease of £40 in Creditors Account only

6 If capital appears on the asset side of the Balance Sheet then the business is
- **A** solvent
- **B** bankrupt
- **C** insolvent
- **D** over-capitalised

7 The financial position of a company at any one point in time is shown in the
- **A** Trading Account
- **B** Profit and Loss Account
- **C** Balance Sheet
- **D** Cash Account

8 The 'sources of funds' is another name for
A liabilities **B** assets **C** capital **D** loans

9 An item, 'Machinery £10 000', in a Balance Sheet of a company means that
- **A** the company owns machinery which cost £10 000
- **B** the company owns machinery which it has valued at £10 000
- **C** the company has spent £10 000 on machinery but it does not have it now
- **D** the company uses a machine worth £10 000 but it does not necessarily own it

10 Which of the following is *not* a fixed asset?
A Premises **B** Machinery **C** Stock **D** Fixtures and fittings

11 Fixed assets are
- **A** assets that are continually changing their value
- **B** assets that cannot easily be turned into cash
- **C** assets that were bought at a fixed price
- **D** assets that the company wishes to use over a long period

12 Current assets are
- **A** assets that are continually changing their value from day to day
- **B** another name for cash
- **C** assets which cannot easily be turned into cash
- **D** assets that can be moved easily

13 Current liabilities are
- **A** long-term liabilities
- **B** ordinary shares
- **C** mortgages with more than 5 years until expiry
- **D** short-term liabilities

14 Working capital is the difference between
- **A** fixed and current liabilities
- **B** current assets and current liabilities
- **C** fixed and current assets
- **D** cash in hand and at bank

15 If a business has no working capital
- **A** it is insolvent
- **B** it is bankrupt
- **C** its activities will be restricted and its financial position harassed
- **D** its activities remain unrestricted

16 In order to obtain more working capital a company could
- **A** sell more goods on credit by reducing the price below cost
- **B** pay as many creditors as possible
- **C** increase stock
- **D** obtain a long-term mortgage on its premises

17 If goods which cost £150 were sold on credit for £200 then
- **A** the Creditors Account will increase by £200 and stock decrease by £200
- **B** the Debtors Account will increase by £200 and the stock decrease by £200
- **C** the stock will decrease by £150, the Debtors Account will increase by £200 and the Capital Account will increase by £50
- **D** the Debtors Account will increase by £200 and the Creditors Account by £150

18 If premises shown in the Balance Sheet at £3000 are revalued at £6000 then
- **A** the Bank Account will also increase by £3000
- **B** the Capital Account will increase by £3000
- **C** creditors will increase by £3000
- **D** there will be no other changes

19 Liquid assets are
- **A** the difference between fixed assets and current assets
- **B** cash and anything that can be turned into cash quickly
- **C** cash only
- **D** the difference between current assets and current liabilities

20 If a company becomes insolvent it
- **A** cannot continue to trade
- **B** can continue to trade but must inform its creditors
- **C** can continue to trade but it is an offence against the law to do so
- **D** has no effect on the company's trading

6
Control accounts

1 Which of the following advantages can be obtained from keeping Control Accounts?
  A Figures for total debtors and creditors can be obtained more easily
  B All the ledgers are self-balancing
  C The Trial Balance can be prepared from the General Ledger only
  D All three of the above

2 The balance on the Sales Ledger Control Account gives the
  A total sales
  B total purchases
  C total debtors
  D difference between debtors and creditors

3 On the Sales Ledger Control Account in the General Ledger
  A there is usually a credit balance
  B there is usually a debit balance
  C there could be either a debit or a credit balance
  D there should be no balance, it should balance itself like a Trial Balance

4 A credit balance on the Sales Ledger Control Account in the General Ledger would arise
  A when a customer has overpaid his account
  B when a customer has returned goods after he had paid his account
  C when a customer failed to take cash discount due
  D under all of the above circumstances

5 The balance in the Purchases Ledger Control Account in the General Ledger is the total of the
  A debtors
  B sales
  C purchases
  D individual balances in the Purchases Ledger

6 In the Purchases Control Account in the General Ledger
- **A** there is usually a credit balance
- **B** there is usually a debit balance
- **C** there could be either a debit or a credit balance
- **D** there should be no balance, it should balance itself like a Trial Balance

7 A debit balance on the Purchases Control Account in the General Ledger could arise
- **A** when a Supplier's Account has been overpaid
- **B** when goods have been returned to a supplier after his account has been paid
- **C** when a supplier has failed to take advantage of cash discount due when paying his account
- **D** in all of the above circumstances

8 In the General Ledger the discounts allowed in the Sales Ledger Control Account will
- **A** appear on the debit side
- **B** appear on the credit side
- **C** not be shown at all
- **D** not be shown in the Sales Control Account but the Purchases Control Account

9 In the General Ledger discounts receivable should be shown on the
- **A** debit of the Sales Ledger Control Account
- **B** credit of the Sales Ledger Control Account
- **C** debit of the Purchases Ledger Control Account
- **D** credit of the Purchases Ledger Control Account

10 A Self-balancing Ledger is one in which
- **A** the total debtors equal the total creditors
- **B** the balances when extracted form a complete Trial Balance
- **C** the total of the balances equals the difference between the creditors and the debtors
- **D** the total number of accounts in the Personal Ledger equals the total number of accounts in the General Ledger

11 Which of the following statements is false? A company keeping Control Accounts
- **A** can extract a Trial Balance from the General Ledger only
- **B** can locate errors more easily
- **C** will know that if the balance on the Control Account agrees with the total of the individual balances then there cannot be a mistake
- **D** can obtain figures of total creditors and debtors more quickly

12 When a Sales Ledger Control Account is maintained in the General Ledger then the entries for posting the total of the Sales Day Book are
- **A** debit Sales Ledger Control Account, credit Sales Account
- **B** credit Sales Ledger Control Account, credit Sales Account
- **C** debit both Sales Account and Sales Ledger Control Account
- **D** credit Sales Ledger Control Account instead of Sales Account

13 When a Purchases Ledger Control Account is maintained in the General Ledger then the entries for posting the total of the Purchases Day Book are

A credit Purchases Ledger Control Account, debit Purchases Account

B credit both Purchases Account and Purchases Ledger Control Account

C debit both Purchases Account and Purchases Ledger Control Account

D debit Purchases Ledger Control Account instead of Purchases Account

14 A company that has been trading for a number of years and whose financial year ends on 31 December decides to introduce Control Accounts on 1 May. The opening balance on the Purchases Ledger Control Account will be obtained

A by totalling the creditors in that ledger

B by totalling the debtors in that ledger

C from the figure for debtors in the last Balance Sheet

D from the figure for creditors in the last Balance Sheet

******

Consider the following Purchases Ledger Control Account then answer questions 15–20.

Purchases Ledger Control Account

19—			£		19—			£	
1 Jan	Balance	b/d	64	00	1 Jan	Balance	b/d	4670	00
31 Jan	Bank		2562	00	31 Jan	Purchases		2742	00
	Sales Ledger control (contra)		102	00					
	Returns		85	00		Balance	c/d	73	00
	Balance	c/d	4672	00					
			7485	00				7485	00
19—					19—				
1 Feb	Balance	b/d	73	00	1 Feb	Balance	b/d	4672	00

15 The reason that the purchases £2742 is posted to the credit of the Control Account is because

A it is the double entry for the total of the Purchases Account

B it represents the total of all purchases both cash and credit

C it represents the total of all the purchases posted to the Personal Accounts in the Personal Accounts Ledger

D it is the amount necessary to balance the account

16 The accounts mainly concerned with this Control Account are
- **A** the Personal Accounts of suppliers
- **B** the Personal Accounts of customers
- **C** Real Accounts
- **D** Nominal Accounts

17 The balance of £4672 represents the total of
- **A** all the credit balances of the business
- **B** all the creditors of the business
- **C** the individual credit balances in the Purchases Ledger
- **D** the individual balances in the Sales Ledger

18 The debit balance of £73 could be due to
- **A** goods returned to a supplier after the account had been paid
- **B** an account being overpaid
- **C** a customer, whose account in the Sales Ledger stood at £102, was also a supplier who had an account of £29 in the Purchases Ledger and these accounts were settled by means of set-off
- **D** all three of the above

19 The entry 'Sales Ledger Control (contra) £102' was
- **A** due to a correction of an error of posting a purchase of £102 to J. Jones instead of I.J. Jones
- **B** the amount necessary to make the Sales Ledger Control Account balance
- **C** the amount necessary to make the Purchases Control Account balance
- **D** an account settled by means of set-off

20 The entry 'Bank £2562' was
- **A** the total amount paid into the bank for January
- **B** the total amount of cheques drawn from the bank for January
- **C** obtained from an analysis column of the debit side of the Cash Book
- **D** obtained from an analysis column of the credit side of the Cash Book

7

Suspense accounts and correction of errors

1 An error of omission is made if
- **A** an entry is made in the wrong account
- **B** a figure is transposed, eg 19 being entered as 91
- **C** a total has been wrongly cast
- **D** a transaction is overlooked completely

2 An error of commission is made if
- **A** a transaction has been overlooked
- **B** an entry is made in the wrong account within the correct class
- **C** a total has been wrongly cast
- **D** an entry has been made on the wrong side of an account

3 An error of principle is made if
- **A** a total has been wrongly cast
- **B** a transaction has been overlooked
- **C** an entry is made to the wrong class of account
- **D** a figure has been transposed

4 A compensating error is made if
- **A** two or more errors cancel each other out
- **B** two accounts have debit balances of the same amount
- **C** two accounts have credit balances of the same amount
- **D** an entry is made in the wrong account

5 Which of these errors will affect the balancing of the Trial Balance?

A Compensating **B** Commission **C** Omission **D** None of these

6 Which of these errors will not affect the balancing of the Trial Balance?
- **A** A compensating error
- **B** Where only a single entry is made
- **C** Where an item is debited instead of credited
- **D** None of these

7 To correct errors entries should first be made in the Journal because
- **A** this completes the double entry
- **B** this provides a record explaining the entries made in the Ledger
- **C** it is easier to do
- **D** it saves entering it in the Ledger

8 Goods sold to S. Smith were debited to S. Smithers' Account. The entries necessary to correct this error will be

A debit S. Smith's Account, credit S. Smithers' Account
B debit S. Smithers' Account, credit S. Smith's Account
C debit Sales Account, credit S. Smith's Account
D debit S. Smithers' Account, credit Sales Account

9 A company purchased goods from S.W. Wholesalers Ltd for £56. This was posted in error to the debit of S.W. Wholesalers Ltd's Account. The entries necessary to correct this error will be

A debit Suspense Account £56 and credit S.W. Wholesalers Ltd £56
B credit S.W. Wholesalers Ltd £112 only
C debit Suspense Account £56 and credit Purchases Account £56
D credit Purchases Account £112 only

10 If a Trial Balance does not balance and it is necessary to prepare the Final Accounts before the error can be found, it will be necessary to post the difference to

A the Capital Account **B** the Drawings Account
C the Suspense Account **D** the Control Account

11 A cheque received from A. Jones for £50 was posted to the debit of A. Jones's Account. The entries necessary to correct this error are

A credit A. Jones's Account £100 only
B debit Bank Account £50 and credit A. Jones's Account £50
C credit A. Jones's Account £50 only
D debit A. Jones's Account £100 only

12 A cheque received from A. Lloyd was posted to the debit of B. Lloyd's Account. The entries necessary to correct this error are

A credit both A. Lloyd and B. Lloyd with the amount of the cheque
B debit B. Lloyd's Account and credit A. Lloyd with the amount of the cheque
C debit B. Lloyd's Account with twice the amount of the cheque and credit A. Lloyd with the amount of the cheque
D debit B. Lloyd's Account with twice the amount of the cheque and credit A. Lloyd with the amount of the cheque

13 Which of these errors will be disclosed by the Trial Balance?

A A cheque received from a debtor for £52 was entered in the Cash Book as £25
B A credit note from a supplier had been overlooked
C Rent received and correctly entered in the Cash Book had been debited to the Rent Account
D Wages paid for installing a new machine were debited to Wages Account

14 A Suspense Account is used

A to provide the double entry when an account needs to be adjusted for payments paid in advance

B when it is necessary to write off a bad debt

C when Final Accounts have to be prepared before a Trial Balance can be balanced

D to record a sale-or-return transaction

15 A Suspense Account shows a debit balance of £40. One of the errors necessitating the opening of a Suspense Account was that the total of £40 of the discounts received column in the Cash Book had been posted to the debit of Discount Account. When this error was found and posted to the Suspense Account, it will have

A no balance

B a debit balance of £120

C a credit balance of £80

D a debit balance of £80

16 The following errors were discovered after the Trial Balance had been balanced by using a Suspense Account.

1 A credit sale of £40 to I. James was posted to the debit of S. James's Account

2 The Sales Day Book was totalled as £650 but should have been £750

3 Rates paid £340 had been posted to the Rates Account as £430

These errors were corrected using the Suspense Account which then balanced. The original balance on this Suspense Account was

A a debit of £10 **B** a credit of £10 **C** a debit of £190

D a credit of £190

17 If the draft Final Accounts of a company have to be prepared before a Trial Balance is balanced, any difference will be shown in a Suspense Account which will appear as

A a liability in the Balance Sheet

B an asset in the Balance Sheet

C either a liability or an asset in the Balance Sheet

D a debit in the Profit and Loss Account

18 If the difference between the totals of the debit and credit sides of a Trial Balance is divisible by 9 then the error is likely to be an

A error of addition

B error due to a transposition of a figure (eg 28 as 82)

C error in posting

D error of omission

19 If the difference between the totals of the sides of a Trial Balance is 1, 10, 100, or 1000 then the error is likely to be

A an error of omission

B a transposed figure

C an error of posting
D an error of addition

20 If an error was made by posting a return to a supplier of goods valued £30 to the credit of the Suppliers Account then the debit side of the Trial Balance would be
A £30 greater than the credit
B £60 greater than the credit
C £60 less than the credit
D £15 less than the credit

8
Bank reconciliation statements

1 A Bank Statement is
 A a detailed statement of all money paid into and taken out of a Bank Current Account
 B a letter stating that a Bank Current Account is overdrawn
 C similar to a banker's order
 D a detailed statement of all direct debits

2 Credit transfers are often in the Bank Statement but on checking are not found in the Cash Book. This is because they are
 A seldom used
 B only used to pay accounts long overdue
 C never entered in the Cash Book
 D not entered in the Paying-in Book

3 A direct debit
 A is a direct payment into another person's Bank Account
 B tells a banker to allow someone else to take a sum of money from one's account on a certain date
 C tells a banker to pay someone else a certain sum of money at regular intervals
 D is similar to bank charges

4 A request to a banker to make payments at regular intervals is known as a
 A direct debit **B** bank giro **C** standing order **D** credit transfer

5 A Bank Reconciliation Statement is a statement
 A received from the bank but with the debits and credits reversed
 B drawn up to verify the balance as per the Cash Book with the balance as per the Bank Statement
 C received from the bank showing how the bank charges are made up
 D issued by the bank to indicate that an account is overdrawn

6 When preparing a Bank Reconciliation Statement a cheque sent to a creditor but not yet presented for payment should be
 A added to the balance as per Cash Book provided the account is not overdrawn
 B added to the balance as per Bank Statement provided that the account is not overdrawn

C ignored

D deducted from the balance as per Cash Book provided the account is not overdrawn

7 If a Current Account is not overdrawn when a Bank Reconciliation Statement is prepared, cheques paid into the bank but not appearing in the Bank Statement should be

A added to the balance as per Cash Book

B added to the balance as per Bank Statement

C ignored

D deducted from the balance as per Bank Statement

8 The balance as per Bank Account in the Cash Book was £200 and as per the Bank Statement £220. The cheques not presented were £30 but bank charges of £10 included in the Bank Statement had not been entered in the Cash Book. The real balance on the Bank Account in the Cash Book will be

A £200 **B** £220 **C** £260 **D** £190

9 It is necessary for a company to prepare a Bank Reconciliation Statement because

A although the Cash Book is always up to date the Bank Statement is not

B the business wishes to avoid an overdraft

C neither the Cash Book nor the Bank Statement are usually up to date

D the Bank Statement is not a true record

10 Which of the following statements is true? The final figure on the Bank Reconciliation Statement

A is never the true balance

B is always the balance as per Cash Book

C is always the balance as per Bank Statement

D could be either the balance as per Cash Book or as per Bank Statement

11 The Bank Statement shows a credit balance of £120. When comparing this statement with the Cash Book it was found that the cheques drawn but not presented for payment amounted to £340 and that there was a standing order for £45 and bank charges of £21 not in the Cash Book. The Cash Book balance will be

A £286 credit **B** £244 credit **C** £295 debit **D** £154 credit

******

Consider the following Cash Book and Bank Statement and then answer questions 12–15

Cash Book
(Bank columns only)

19—			£		19—			£	
1 June	Balance	b/d	286	00	2 June	W. Morgan		129	00
9 June	Sales		267	00	7 June	T. Smith		176	00
	P. Peters		302	00	10 June	Rent		214	00
11 June	Sales		313	00	14 June	R. Rowlands		97	00
12 June	L. Lloyd		246	00	15 June	Wages		285	00
15 June	Sales		328	00	19 June	Higgins		65	00
27 June	P. Peters		58	00	25 June	R. Rowlands		143	00
30 June	Sales		373	00	30 June	Wages		265	00
						Balance	c/d	799	00
			2173	00				2173	00
1 July	Balance	b/d	799	00					

Bank Statement

19—		Dr.		Cr.	Balance	
1 June	Balance				328	00
2 June	509	42	00		286	00
9 June	Sundries			569 00	855	00
10 June	512	129	00		726	00
11 June	Sundries			313 00	1039	00
14 June	Sundries			246 00	1285	00
15 June	516	285	00		1000	00
18 June	Sundries			328 00	1328	00
19 June	SO	10	00		1318	00
23 June	517	65	00		1253	00
26 June	Charges	25	00		1228	00
30 June	519	265	00		963	00
	514	214	00		749	00
	513	176	00		573	00

12 The total of the cheques not yet presented for payment is
A £97 + £143 = £240 **C** £58 + £373 = £431
B £129 + £10 + £25 = £164 **D** £42 + £97 + £143 = £282

13 The total amount not credited in the Bank Statement is
A £97 + £143 = £240
B £286 + £58 + £373 = £717
C £58 + £373 = £431
D £10 + £25 = £35

14 What should be the correct balance in the Cash Book?
A £799 **B** £573 **C** £834 **D** £764

15 Why is the cheque for R. Rowlands for £143 not shown in the Bank Statement?
A Because no cheques are cleared between 25 and 30 June every year
B Because the cheque was drawn on a Sunday
C Because the cheque was crossed
D Because it had not been presented for payment before 30 June

16 Why do the dates of some entries in the Cash Book and Bank Statement differ?
A Because banks write up their clients' accounts only once a week
B Because it sometimes takes a few days to clear a cheque
C In order to give clients time to stop a cheque
D In case some cheques may be dishonoured

17 If a Bank Statement shows an overdraft when reconciling it with the Cash Book, any cheques paid but not yet presented for payment
A need not be considered as the account is overdrawn already
B must be added to the Bank Statement balance
C must be deducted from the Bank Statement balance
D must be added to both the Cash Book and Bank Statement balances

18 Standing orders are
A regular payments made by a bank for their clients
B similar to postal orders
C regular orders for the sale of goods
D the same as order cheques

19 The Bank Statement shows a credit balance of £135. When preparing a Bank Reconciliation Statement it is found that cheques drawn but not yet presented for payment amount to £263 and that there is a standing order for £7 in the Bank Statement but not in the Cash Book. What was the original balance in the Cash Book?
A £121 credit **B** £128 credit **C** £405 debit **D** £391 credit

20 Bank charges usually have to be taken into consideration when compiling a Bank Reconciliation Statement because
A banks make charges only when sending out statements
B banks do not usually inform their clients in any other way than through the Bank Statement
C bank charges are never entered in the Cash Book
D bank charges need not be paid

9

Bad debts and provision for bad debts

1 When it is evident that a business cannot collect a debt, the entries necessary for writing off this bad debt will be
- **A** debit Sales Account, credit Personal Account
- **B** debit Bank Account, credit Personal Account
- **C** debit Bad Debts Account, credit Personal Account
- **D** credit Personal Account only

2 P. Peters who owes L. Lewis £100 is bankrupt and a first and final dividend of 25p in the pound is received. The entries to record this in the books of L. Lewis will be
- **A** debit Bank Account £25 and credit P. Peters' Account £25, debit Bad Debts Account £75 and credit P. Peters' Account £75
- **B** debit Bad Debts Account £100, credit P. Peters' Account £100
- **C** debit Bad Debts Account £25 and debit Bank Account £75, credit P. Peters' Account £75
- **D** debit Bank Account £100, credit P. Peters' Account £100

3 When preparing Final Accounts the balance on the Bad Debts Account is closed by a transfer to
- **A** Trading Account
- **B** Profit and Loss Account
- **C** Sales Account
- **D** Capital Account

4 When preparing Final Accounts any bad debts appearing in the Trial Balance will be on the
- **A** credit side and debited to Profit and Loss Account
- **B** credit side and credited to Profit and Loss Account
- **C** debit side and deducted from the debtors in the Balance Sheet
- **D** debit side and be debited to Profit and Loss Account

5 When bad debts are given as an adjustment to the Trial Balance, on preparing Final Accounts the bad debts will be
- **A** deducted from debtors in the Balance Sheet only
- **B** debited to Profit and Loss Account only
- **C** debited to Profit and Loss Account and shown in the Balance Sheet as a liability
- **D** debited to Profit and Loss Account and deducted from the debtors in the Balance Sheet

6 A provision for bad and doubtful debts is created
- **A** to cancel a particular bad debt
- **B** to provide for possible bad debts
- **C** when a debtor becomes bankrupt
- **D** when debts are outstanding for more than two months

7 The entries necessary to make a Provision for Bad and Doubtful Debts Account are
- **A** debit Profit and Loss Account, credit Personal Account
- **B** debit Bad Debts Account, credit Provision for Bad and Doubtful Debts Account
- **C** debit Profit and Loss Account, credit Provision for Bad and Doubtful Debts Account
- **D** debit Provision for Bad and Doubtful Debts Account, credit Profit and Loss Account

8 The balance on the Provision for Bad and Doubtful Debts Account will
- **A** appear in the Trial Balance as a debit
- **B** appear in the Trial Balance as a credit
- **C** not appear in the Trial Balance
- **D** be transferred to the Personal Account concerned

9 The total of debts outstanding is £3000 and it is required to create a Provision for Bad and Doubtful Debts Account equal to 5% of the total of debts outstanding. The entries necessary to create this provision are
- **A** debit Profit and Loss Account £150, credit Bad Debts Account £150
- **B** debit all Personal Accounts with 5% of their balances, credit Provision for Bad and Doubtful Debts Account £150
- **C** debit Provision for Bad and Doubtful Debts Account £150, credit Personal Accounts with 5% of their balances
- **D** debit Profit and Loss Account £150, credit Provision for Bad and Doubtful Debts Account £150

10 The Trial Balance shows the total of debts outstanding £5000 and provision for bad and doubtful debts £120. When preparing Final Accounts it is required to maintain the provision at 5% of the total of debts outstanding. The entries necessary for this are
- **A** debit Profit and Loss Account, credit Provision for Bad and Doubtful Debts Account £250
- **B** debit Provision for Bad and Doubtful Debts Account £250, credit Profit and Loss Account £250
- **C** debit Profit and Loss Account, credit Provision for Bad and Doubtful Debts Account £130
- **D** debit Provision for Bad and Doubtful Debts Account £130, credit Profit and Loss Account £130

11 The Trial Balance shows the total of debts outstanding £4000 and Provision for Bad and Doubtful Debts Account £140. It is required to maintain this provision at 5% of the total of debts outstanding. This provision will be shown in the Balance Sheet as

A a liability of £140
B a deduction of £140 from the total of debts outstanding
C a liability of £200
D a deduction of £200 from the total of debts outstanding

12 It is required to maintain the provision for bad and doubtful debts at 5% of the total of debts outstanding. The present provision stands at £300 and the total of debts outstanding £5000. The entries necesary to record this will be

A debit Profit and Loss Account £50, credit Provision for Bad and Doubtful Debts Account £50
B debit Provision for Bad and Doubtful Debts Account £50, credit Profit and Loss Account £50
C debit Profit and Loss Account £250, credit Provision for Bad and Doubtful Debts Account £250
D debit Provision for Bad and Doubtful Debts Account £250, credit Profit and Loss Account £250

13 On 1 January 19— the Provision for Bad and Doubtful Debts Account showed a balance of £70. The bad debts incurred during the year amounted to £96. On 31 December 19— the total of debts outstanding was £2000. It is required to maintain the Provision for Bad and Doubtful Debts Account at 5% of the total debts outstanding. The entries to record this will be

A debit Profit and Loss Account £100, credit Provision for Bad and Doubtful Debts Account £100
B debit Bad Debts Account £96, credit Provision for Bad and Doubtful Debts Account £96
C debit Profit and Loss Account £126, credit Provision for Bad and Doubtful Debts Account £30 and Bad Debts Account £96
D debit Profit and Loss Account £96 and Bad Debts Account £30, credit Provision for Bad and Doubtful Debts Account £126

14 A Trial Balance shows debtors £2600 and a provision for bad and doubtful debts £60. After the Trial Balance had been extracted it was decided to write off £60 as bad debts and make the provision for bad and doubtful debts up to 5% of the debtors. The new provision will be

A £67 **B** £127 **C** £130 **D** £60

15 One of the reasons for creating a Provision for Bad and Doubtful Debts Account is

A to be able to show the debtors at a more realistic figure in the Balance Sheet
B to cancel any debts outstanding for more than three years
C to encourage debtors to pay promptly
D to give more working capital

16 When a bad debt written off is later recovered the amount received will be

A debited to Provision for Bad and Doubtful Debts Account and credited to Bad Debts Account

B debited to Provision for Bad Debts Account and credited to Bank Account

C debited to Bank Account and credited to Bad Debts Recovered Account

D debited to Bad Debts Recovered Account and credited to Bank Account

17 A company makes provision for bad and doubtful debts equal to 5% of the total of debts outstanding. On 1 January 19— the provision stood at £350 and on 31 December 19— the total of debts outstanding was £8000, on 31 December 19-1 £10 400 and on 31 December 19-2, £12 500. The provision for bad and doubtful debts to be charged to Profit and Loss for the three years ended 31 December 19—, 19-1, and 19-2 will be

	31 December		
	19—	19-1	19-2
A	£350	£ 52	£626
B	£ 50	£120	£105
C	£400	£520	£625
D	£ 50	£170	£275

18 A company's Balance Sheet as at 31 March 19— showed

Total of outstanding debts	£9000
less Provision for bad debts	450
	£8550

At 31 March 19-1 the total of debts outstanding was £10 400 and the bad debts written off during the year were £550. Using the same percentage of debtors for the provision, the total amount of both bad debts and provision for bad and doubtful debts to be debited to Profit and Loss Account will be

A £620 **B** £1000 **C** £1070 **D** £520

19 The Trial Balance shows provision for bad and doubtful debts £325 and debtors £6000. It is required to maintain the provision at 5% of debtors. When preparing Final Accounts, the provision for bad debts will be shown as a

A debit £300 in the Profit and Loss Account whilst the total debts outstanding will be shown in the Balance Sheet £6000 *less* provision for bad debts £300

B debit £25 in the Profit and Loss Account whilst the total debtors outstanding will be shown in the Balance Sheet £6000 *less* provision for bad debts £300

C credit £25 in the Profit and Loss Account whilst the total debtors outstanding will be shown in the Balance Sheet £6000 *less* provision for bad debts £300

D debit £25 in the Profit and Loss Account whilst the total debts outstanding will be shown in the Balance Sheet £6000 *less* provision for bad debts £325

20 A Trial Balance shows 'Provision for bad and doubtful debts £190' and 'Total of debts outstanding £6800'. It is required to write off a further £320 as bad debts and maintain the provision at $2\frac{1}{2}\%$ of the total of debts outstanding. When preparing the Profit and Loss Account the entries will be

A debit £320, credit £20
B debit £320, credit £28
C £490 credit only
D £394 credit only

10
Depreciation

1 Depreciation is
  A a sum of money put aside to replace an asset
  B a charge for wear and tear of an asset
  C the cost of replacing an asset
  D a method of showing less profit than there really should have been
2 Which of the following is *not* a method of depreciation?
  A Fixed instalment
  B Reducing balance
  C Straight line
  D Capitalisation
3 Which of the following is *not* a cause of depreciation?
  A Wear and tear
  B Loss of value as a result of use
  C Obsolescence
  D Revaluation
4 The straight-line method of depreciation is
  A a fixed percentage of the cost each year
  B an estimated amount each year
  C a fixed percentage of the value of the asset at the end of the year
  D an increase in the value of an asset
5 A machine which cost £2000 is expected to last 10 years when its value is expected to be £300. What annual amount should be charged for depreciation using the straight-line method?
  A £200 **B** £300 **C** £170 **D** £250
6 Using the reducing balance method, a car which cost £6000 is depreciated by 20% per annum. What is the written down value of the car at the end of its second year?
  A £4800 **B** £3600 **C** £3840 **D** None of these
7 A van which cost £6000 is depreciated by 20% per annum using the diminishing balance method. The entries for the first year will be
  A debit Depreciation Account £120, credit Profit and Loss Account £120
  B debit Profit and Loss Account £60, credit Depreciation Account £60

C debit Depreciation Account £1200, credit Van Account £1200
D debit Van Account £1200, credit Depreciation Account £1200

8 Appreciation is
A loss due to obsolescence
B loss due to passage of time
C another name for revaluation
D the permanent increase in the value of an asset

9 If loose tools costing £400 are revalued at £430 then the additional £30 will be
A depreciation
B appreciation
C a provision for depreciation
D depreciation reserve

10 When all the assets have been depreciated for the year, the Depreciation Account is
A closed by transfer to Profit and Loss Account
B left open and shown in the Balance Sheet
C closed by transfer to Capital Account
D left open but not shown in the Balance Sheet

11 If it is required to maintain an asset in the books at its original cost then
A the straight-line method of depreciation must be used
B depreciation must be shown only in the Depreciation Account
C a Provision for Depreciation Account must be kept
D the asset must be revalued

12 The method used for depreciating leasehold premises is usually the
A straight-line
B reducing balance
C revaluation
D depletion unit

13 The entries necessary to maintain a Provision for Depreciation Account are
A debit Asset Account, credit Profit and Loss Account
B debit Asset Account, credit Provision for Depreciation Account
C debit Provision for Depreciation Account, credit Profit and Loss Account
D debit Profit and Loss Account, credit Provision for Depreciation Account

14 At the end of the financial period the balance on the Provision for Depreciation Account is
A transferred to the Relative Asset Account
B kept as an open account and deducted from the asset in the Balance Sheet
C transferred to Profit and Loss Account
D transferred to Depreciation Account

15 The balance on the Provision for Depreciation Account shown in the Trial Balance

A is a debit
B is a credit
C can be either a debit or a credit
D is included in the balance on the Bad Debts Account

16 A lorry costing £12 000 was depreciated by 25% per annum using the diminishing balance method. Two years later it was sold for £6000. The profit or loss made on the transaction was

A £750 loss **B** nil **C** £6000 loss **D** £750 profit

17 The Trial Balance shows machinery £5000 and a provision for depreciation on machinery £2640. It is required to depreciate the machinery by a further 20% on cost. When the Balance Sheet is prepared the net value of the machinery shown will be

A £4000 **B** £1000 **C** £2360 **D** £1360

18 The method of depreciation used to avoid complications when additions or sales of an asset are numerous is the

A straight-line
B diminishing balance
C revaluation
D equal instalment

19 The Plant and Machinery Account has a balance of £45 000 and the Provision for Depreciation Account £22 000. A machine which was bought two years previously for £14 000 was sold for £5000. The Plant and Machinery Account has been depreciated at 20% per annum on cost. The balance on the Provision for Depreciation Account after this sale will be

A £22 000 **B** £16 000 **C** £16 400 **D** £400

20 Using the information in question 19 above, the balance on the Plant and Machinery Account after the sale will be

A £39 000 **B** £31 000 **C** £36 600 **D** £23 000

11
The accounts of clubs and societies

1 A Receipts and Payments Account is
  A similar to a Profit and Loss Account
  B a summarised Cash and Bank Account
  C another name for a Statement of Affairs
  D similar to a Balance Sheet

2 A Receipts and Payments Account shows
  A the actual receipts and payments made during a period
  B what the receipts and payments should have been
  C the Accumulated Fund
  D the profit or loss

3 The balance on the Receipts and Payments Account is
  A the profit or loss for the period
  B the amount owing to or by the club or society
  C the balance on the Cash or Bank Accounts
  D the amount of subscriptions received

4 The Income and Expenditure Account is similar to a
  A Balance Sheet
  B Cash Account
  C Capital Account
  D Trading and Profit and Loss Account

5 The balance on the Income and Expenditure Account is the
  A amount of cash in hand
  B profit or loss for the period
  C accumulated fund
  D subscriptions due

6 The items in the Income and Expenditure Account show
  A all amounts actually received or paid during the period
  B all amounts which should have been received or paid during the period
  C only the actual revenue receipts or payments for the period
  D only the revenue receipts or payments which should have been received or paid during the period

7 The Accumulated Fund is another name for
  A the profit **B** total assets **C** capital **D** working capital

8 A deficit is the same as
  A a loss

B an overdraft
C a credit balance on the Income and Expenditure Account
D a debit balance on the Receipts and Payments Account

9 The profit of a club or society is often referred to as a
A donation **B** surplus **C** subscription in advance **D** deficit

10 Subscriptions received in advance are
A included in the 'Subscriptions' entry when preparing an Income and Expenditure Account
B not included in a Receipts and Payments Account
C shown on the asset side of the Balance Sheet
D shown in the Balance Sheet as a liability

11 The purchase of a lawnmower is shown in the
A Receipts and Payments Account only
B Receipts and Payments Account and the Balance Sheet
C Income and Expenditure Account and the Balance Sheet
D Income and Expenditure Account, the Receipts and Payments Account and the Balance Sheet

12 Which is the odd one out?
A Profit
B Surplus
C Credit balance on the Income and Expenditure Account
D Credit balance on the Receipts and Payments Account

13 Which is the odd one out?
A Cash in hand
B A debit balance on the Receipts and Payments Account
C A credit balance on the Income and Expenditure Account
D A debit balance on the Cash Account

******

Consider the following Receipts and Payments Account together with the information which follows and then answer questions 14–20.

Receipts and Payments Account
(for year ended 31 December 19—)

Receipts	£		*Payments*	£	
Balance 1 Jan 19—	104	00	Wages	4 600	00
			Repairs	152	00
Subscriptions (this year)	4 202	00	Post and stationery	58	00
			Rent	1 500	00
			Light and Heat	320	00
Subscriptions (last year)	100	00	Payments to bar suppliers	4 280	00
			New bar furniture	500	00
Bar takings	7 040	00	Balance 31 Dec 19—	36	00
	11 446	00		11 446	00

The secretary stated that on 1 January 19— the club owned its own premises valued at £10 000 and fixtures and fittings £1200. The value of the bar stock on 1 January 19— was £460 but it owed £340 for bar supplies. On 31 December 19— subscriptions due to the club amounted to £130 and the value of the bar stock at this date was £420 but it owed £326 to its bar suppliers and £80 for rent.

14 The bar profit for the year was
A £2760 **B** £2800 **C** £2720 **D** £2734

15 The Income and Expenditure Account will show subscriptions as
A £4332 **B** £4202 **C** £4072 **D** £4302

16 The Accumulated Fund on 1 January 19— will be
A £11 524 **B** £11 420 **C** £11 760 **D** £11 864

17 The balance on the Income and Expenditure Account on 31 December 19— will be
A £436 surplus **C** £226 surplus
B £356 surplus **D** £544 deficit

18 The total of fixed assets on 31 December 19— will be
A £11 700 **B** £11 200 **C** £10 000 **D** £10 420

19 The total of current assets on 31 December 19— will be
A £550 **B** £1050 **C** £166 **D** £586

20 The Accumulated Fund on 31 December 19— will be
A £11 880 **B** £11 524 **C** £11 864 **D** £12 220

12
Manufacturing accounts

1 Prime cost is
- **A** cost of raw materials used
- **B** cost of raw materials used plus direct labour and direct expenses
- **C** cost of raw materials used plus factory overheads
- **D** another name for factory overheads

2 Purchases of raw materials plus raw materials at the start less stock of raw materials at the end of a period is the
- **A** prime cost
- **B** value of work in progress
- **C** cost of raw materials used
- **D** net cost of production

3 Which of the following is *not* a factory overhead?
- **A** Depreciation of machinery
- **B** Storekeepers' wages
- **C** Wages of operatives
- **D** Sales representatives' commission

4 Work in progress is the
- **A** cost of production
- **B** value of the goods produced
- **C** value of finished goods on hand
- **D** value of partly finished goods

5 The net cost of production is
- **A** prime cost plus factory overheads, plus work in progress at the start of the period, less work in progress at the end of the period
- **B** prime cost plus factory overheads
- **C** same as gross profit
- **D** same as net profit

******

Consider the following information and then answer questions 6–9.

	1 Jan 19—	31 Dec 19—
	£	£
Stock of raw materials	10 000	12 000
Work in progress	16 000	17 000
Stock of finished goods	14 400	15 400

Some other balances for the year ended 31 December 19— were: factory rent £5000, machinery repairs £2680, Works Manager's salary £14 000, salaries £25 600, factory wages £51 600, purchases of raw materials £28 800.

6 The cost of raw materials used will be
A £28 800 **B** £38 800 **C** £16 800 **D** £26 800

7 The prime cost will be
A £78 400 **B** £38 800 **C** £83 200 **D** £85 880

8 The net works cost of production of finished goods will be
A £100 080 **B** £85 880 **C** £99 080 **D** £125 600

9 The total of the factory overheads will be
A £56 600 **B** £21 680 **C** £47 280 **D** £64 280

******

Consider the following Manufacturing Account and then answer questions 10–12

Manufacturing Account
(for the year ended 31 December 19—)

	£	£
Stock of raw materials 1 Jan 19—		67 800
Purchases of raw materials		976 000
		1 043 800
less Stock of raw materials 31 Dec 19—		79 000
		964 800
Direct wages		1 056 200
		2 021 000
Factory overheads		
Indirect wages	74 000	
Indirect materials	11 200	
Factory heat, light & power	25 000	
Factory rent and rates	24 000	
Depreciation of machinery	36 000	170 200
		2 191 200
add Work in progress 1 Jan 19—		84 000
		2 275 000
less Work in progress 31 Dec 19—		92 100
		2 183 100

10 The cost of finished goods manufactured will be
A £2 021 000 **B** £2 191 200 **C** £2 183 100 **D** £964 800

11 The prime cost will be
A £2 021 000 **B** £2 191 200 **C** £2 183 100 **D** £170 200

12 The cost of raw materials used will be
A £2 021 000 **B** £964 800 **C** £170 200 **D** £2 191 200

13 If the stock of finished goods at the start of a period was valued at £76 500 and at the end of the period £79 700 and the cost of goods manufactured was £1 065 200, then the cost of the goods sold will be
A £1 065 200 **B** £1 068 400 **C** £1 221 400 **D** £1 062 000

14 Using the information in question 13 above, if the sales for the period were £2 125 000 then the gross profit will be
A £1 059 800 **B** £1 056 600 **C** £1 903 600 **D** £1 063 000

15 Which of the following is an administrative expense?
A Carriage outwards **C** Sales representatives' commission
B Depreciation of vans **D** Loan interest

16 Which of the following is a selling expense?
A Advertising **C** Loan interest
B Office salaries **D** Carriage outwards

17 Which of the following is a distributive expense?
A Office salaries **C** Carriage outwards
B Advertising **D** Factory foreman's wages

18 Which of the following is an indirect factory expense?
A Carriage inwards **C** Office salaries
B Factory foreman's wages **D** Advertising

19 Which of the following is a direct expense?
A Factory foreman's wages **C** Royalties
B Carriage outwards **D** Office salaries

20 The difference between direct and indirect expenses is
A direct expenses are a prime cost but indirect expenses are factory overheads
B direct expenses are factory overheads but indirect expenses are a prime cost
C direct expenses vary directly with wages but indirect expenses have no relation to wages
D direct expenses are directly concerned with production but indirect expenses are only partly concerned with production

13
Partnerships

1 If there is no partnership deed then profits and losses

A can be divided just as the partners wish

B must be shared equally

C must be shared in proportion to the percentage of capital invested

D must be shared equally, after an adjustment for interest on capitals has been made

2 If there is no partnership agreement, which statement is *untrue*?

A Profits and losses can be shared equally

B No interest can be claimed on capitals

C No partner can claim a wage or salary for working in the business

D No partnership exists

3 When it is required to maintain fixed capitals then any share of profits must be

A credited to Capital Accounts

B debited to Capital Accounts

C credited to Partners' Current Accounts

D debited to Partners' Current Accounts

4 In a partnership where capitals are fixed, an item in the Profit and Loss Account (Appropriation Section) shows a partner's salary as £10 000. The double entry for this will be a

A debit in the Profit and Loss Account

B credit in the Capital Account of the partner concerned

C debit in the Current Account of the partner concerned

D credit in the Current Account of the partner concerned

5 In a partnership where fixed capitals are maintained

A shares of profits, partners' salaries and partners' interest on capitals will be credited to respective Capital Accounts

B shares of profits, partners' salaries and partners' interest on capitals will be debited to Profit and Loss Account (Appropriation Section)

C shares of profits will be credited to the respective Partners' Current Accounts but the partners' salaries and interest on capital will be credited to the respective Capital Accounts

D the partners' shares of profits will be credited to the respective Capital Accounts but the partners' salaries and interest on capital will be credited to the respective Partners' Current Accounts

6 X and Y are in partnership and share profits and losses in the ratio $\frac{3}{5} : \frac{2}{5}$. The net profit is £26 000. X is to receive a salary of £6000. The partners' shares of the profit will be

A X £13 000, Y £13 000 **C** X £18 000, Y £8000
B X £11 600, Y £10 400 **D** X £12 000, Y £8000

7 Using the information in question 6 above, the amounts to be credited to Partners' Current Accounts will be

A X £14 000, Y £13 000 **C** X £18 000, Y £8000
B X £11 000, Y £10 400 **D** X £12 000, Y £8000

8 In the Trial Balance, Partners' Current Accounts

A are always shown on the credit side
B are always shown on the debit side
C can be shown on either side
D are never shown

9 When there is a credit balance on a Partner's Current Account then

A the partner has drawn out more than his share of profit
B the partner owes the partnership
C there is a bank overdraft
D the partner has not drawn out his full share of profits

10 Where fixed capitals are maintained then partners' drawings are transferred to the

A credit of Capital Accounts
B debit of Capital Accounts
C credit of Partners' Current Accounts
D debit of Partners' Current Accounts

11 Where interest is charged on drawings then the entries will be

A debit Profit and Loss Account (Appropriation Section), credit Partners' Current Accounts
B debit Profit and Loss Account (Appropriation Section), credit Partners' Capital Account
C debit Partners' Capital Account, credit Profit and Loss Account (Appropriation Section)
D debit Partners' Current Account, credit Profit and Loss Account (Appropriation Section)

******

Consider the following Profit and Loss Appropriation Account and then answer questions 12–17.

Baron and Earl are in partnership sharing profits and losses equally. At the start of the year the balances on the Partners' Current Accounts were: Baron £220 credit, Earl £192 debit. The drawings for the year were: Baron £6000, Earl £8000. The Profit and Loss Appropriation Account for the year is shown below.

Profit and Loss Appropriation Account
(for year ended 31 December 19—)

	£		£
Interest on capital (Baron)	1 000 00	Net profit	15 000 00
Interest on capital (Earl)	500 00		
Partner's salary (Earl)	3 300 00		
Share of profits (Baron)	5 100 00		
Share of profits (Earl)	5 100 00		
	15 000 00		15 000 00

12 The balance on Baron's Current Account will be
A £40 debit **B** £40 credit **C** £180 debit **D** £320 credit

13 The balance on Earl's Current Account will be
A £708 debit **B** £708 credit **C** £1064 debit **D** £1064 credit

14 If no partnership agreement exists then Baron's share of the profits will be
A £5100 **B** £8400 **C** £5000 **D** £7500

15 If no partnership agreement exists then Earl's share of the profits will be
A £7500 **B** £5100 **C** £8400 **D** £5000

16 If no partnership agreement exists then the balance on Baron's Current Account will be
A £1720 credit **B** £1720 debit **C** £1280 credit **D** £1280 debit

17 If no partnership agreement exists then the balance on Earl's Current Account will be
A £208 debit **B** £692 debit **C** £208 credit **D** £308 credit

******

Consider the following Current Account and then answer questions 18–20.

Rose: Current Account

19—			£		19—			£	
31 Jan	Drawings		16 000	00	1 Jan	Balance	b/d	480	00
	Interest on drawings		80	00		Wages		10 000	00
31 Dec	Balance	c/d	2 000	00		Interest on capital		560	00
						Share of profit		7 040	00
			18 080	00				18 080	00
					19–1				
					1 Jan	Balance	b/d	2 000	00

18 The balance on 1 January 19–1 means
- **A** that Rose has not drawn his full entitlement
- **B** that Rose owes the firm £2000
- **C** that Rose's real share of the profit was £7040 – £2000 = £5040
- **D** none of the above

19 The double entry for wages will be found in the
- **A** Capital Account (Rose)
- **B** Profit and Loss Appropriation Account
- **C** Cash or Bank Accounts
- **D** Profit and Loss Account

20 The amount of money or money's worth that Rose actually took out from the partnership during the year was
A £18 000 **B** £17 480 **C** £16 000 **D** £16 080

14
Company accounts

1 The profit made by a limited company
- **A** is added to the Capital Account
- **B** is paid out to the shareholders in the form of dividends
- **C** is divided so that some is shared out as dividends and the remainder is added to capital
- **D** is divided so that some is shared out as dividends and the remainder is shown as a reserve in the Balance Sheet

2 The fees of the directors of a limited company are
- **A** debited to Trading Account
- **B** debited to Profit and Loss Account
- **C** treated in the same way as drawings and deducted from the capital
- **D** credited to Profit and Loss Account

3 Revenue reserves are
- **A** profits which cannot be distributed as dividends
- **B** undistributed profits that can be applied in any way the directors wish
- **C** profits arising from capital gains
- **D** reserves set aside for a particular purpose

4 Capital reserves are
- **A** reserves arising out of capital gains
- **B** equal to the balance on Profit and Loss Account
- **C** undistributed profits
- **D** ordinary dividends

5 Dividends
- **A** must be declared whenever profits are made
- **B** can be declared whenever the directors wish
- **C** can only be paid when profits are made
- **D** must be at least 5% per annum

6 The authorised share capital of a limited company is
- **A** the total amount issued to shareholders
- **B** the total amount paid up by shareholders
- **C** the amount mentioned in the Memorandum of Association
- **D** the same as ordinary share capital

7 The issued capital of a limited company is
A always the same as the authorised capital
B the total value of the shares issued to shareholders at the issue price
C the total amount paid by shareholders for their shares
D the same as preference share capital

8 Debentures are
A the same as ordinary shares
B the same as preference shares
C certificates showing that loans have been made to the company
D shares which cannot be paid back to the shareholders

9 When a company has issued debentures, the interest due is debited to Profit and Loss Account
A only when it has been paid
B only when there is a profit
C only when the directors wish
D whether a profit or a loss has been made

10 Which is the odd one out?
A Preference shares **C** Equities
B Ordinary shares **D** Debentures

11 A limited company's net profit is £36 000. It has 40 000 10% preference shares of £1 each and 400 000 ordinary shares of £1 each. The directors decide to set aside £8000 for general reserves. What is the maximum percentage dividend that can be paid to ordinary shareholders?
A 10% **B** 5% **C** 8% **D** 6%

******

Consider the following extract from a company's Balance Sheet and then answer questions 12–15.

	£
400 000 ordinary shares of £1 each	400 000
40 000 10% preference shares of £1 each	40 000
Share premium	8 000
General reserves	56 000
Profit and Loss Account	12 000
6% debentures	24 000
Trade creditors	18 000
Proposed dividends	44 000
	602 000

12 What is the total of the share capital?
A £400 000 **B** £424 000 **C** £440 000 **D** £484 000

13 What is the total of the capital reserves?
A £64 000 **B** £8000 **C** £76 000 **D** £12 000

14 What is the total of the revenue reserve?
A £36 000 **B** £8000 **C** £12 000 **D** £68 000

15 What is the total of loan capital?
A £600 000 **B** £464 000 **C** £86 000 **D** £24 000

16 The Trial Balance of a limited company whose capital is £400 000, divided into 400 000 ordinary shares of £1 each, showed a credit balance on its Profit and Loss Account £12 800. The net profit for the year was £52 000. The directors decide to set aside £8000 for general reserves and make a distribution of 10% to ordinary shareholders. After these transactions are completed the balance on the Profit and Loss Account in the Balance Sheet will be
A £16 800 **B** £12 000 **C** £24 800 **D** £12 800

17 Which of the following items should *not* appear in the Appropriation Section of the Profit and Loss Account?
A Debenture interest
B General reserve
C Proposed dividends
D Balance on Profit and Loss Account

18 When shares are sold 'at par' it means they are sold for
A their market value
B their nominal value
C their value at the time of issue
D £1 each

19 When shares are sold at a discount it means that they are sold
A subject to a cash discount for prompt payment
B for more than their par value
C for less than their par value
D for less than their market value

20 When shares are sold at a premium it means that the price is
A more than their par value
B less than their par value
C more than their market value
D less than their market value

15
Goodwill. The purchase of a business

1 The difference between the purchase price and the net value of a business is known as
A capital **B** profit **C** goodwill **D** working capital

2 If a business whose assets are valued at £84 000 had liabilities of £12 000 and is sold for £90 000 then the value of the goodwill will be
A £90 000 **B** £84 000 **C** £18 000 **D** £6000

3 When a business is purchased then the value of the goodwill will appear in the books of the purchaser
A in the Profit and Loss Account as an expense
B in the Balance Sheet deducted from current assets
C as a liability in the Balance Sheet
D as an asset in the Balance Sheet

4 When a business is purchased, in the books of the purchaser the entries for the agreed price are
A debit Purchase of Business Account, credit Vendor's Account
B debit Vendor's Account, credit Purchase of Business Account
C debit Bank Account, credit Purchase of Business Account
D debit Purchase of Business Account, credit Bank Account

5 When a business is purchased, to record the assets in the books of the purchaser the necessary entries will be
A debit Bank Account, credit respective Asset Accounts
B debit respective Asset Accounts, credit Purchase of Business Account
C debit respective Asset Accounts, credit Vendor's Account
D debit Purchase of Business Account, credit respective Asset Accounts

6 When a business is purchased, the entries necessary in the purchaser's books to record the creditors taken over will be
A debit respective Personal Accounts of the creditors, credit Bank Account
B debit Bank Account, credit respective Personal Accounts of the creditors
C debit Purchase of Business Account, credit respective Personal Accounts of the creditors
D debit respective Personal Accounts of the creditors, credit Purchase of Business Account

7 The balance on the Purchase of Business Account is
A the amount owing to the vendor
B the net value of the assets
C working capital
D goodwill

8 East and West are in partnership sharing profits and losses equally. Their Balance Sheet as at 31 December 19— shows 'Capital (East) £15 000' and 'Capital (West) £10 000'. On 1 January 19–1 they decide to admit North as an additional partner but before doing so they introduce Goodwill valued at £10 000. The entries necessary to record this Goodwill will be
A debit Goodwill Account £10 000, credit Capital Account (East) £6000 and Capital Account (West) £4000
B debit Goodwill Account £10 000, credit Current Account (East) £5000 and Current Account (West) £5000
C debit Goodwill Account £10 000, credit Capital Account (East) £5000 and Capital Account (West) £5000
D debit Goodwill Account £10 000, credit Current Account (East) £6000 and Current Account (West) £4000

******

Earl and Duke decide to purchase the business of W. King and prepare a Purchase of Business Account as follows:

Purchase of Business Account

	£			£	
W. King	225 000	00	Sundry assets	250 000	00
Creditors	47 500	00	Goodwill	22 500	00
	272 500	00		272 500	00

Consider the account above and then answer questions 9–12.

9 The price to be paid to W. King for the business is
A £225 000 **B** £250 000 **C** £272 500 **D** £22 500

10 The value of the goodwill was most probably arrived at by
A taking 9% of the sundry assets
B taking 10% of the purchase price
C using the balance of the Purchase of Business Account
D agreement between the vendor, W. King, and the purchasers, Earl and Duke

11 The creditors are to be paid
A by the vendors
B by the purchasers
C half by the vendors and half by the purchasers
D by W. King

12 In the books of Earl and Duke the goodwill
- **A** must be written off immediately to Profit and Loss Account
- **B** will appear in the Balance Sheet as an asset until written off
- **C** will appear as a liability in the Balance Sheet until written off
- **D** will appear only in the Purchase of Business Account

13 Which is the *incorrect* statement? Goodwill can be raised in the books of a business only if it has been
- **A** purchased
- **B** raised in connection with the admission of a new partner
- **C** raised to arrive at the true value of a business on the death of a partner
- **D** raised in order to prevent the Balance Sheet showing the business to be insolvent

14 T. Rees on purchasing a business has agreed to pay goodwill equal to twice the average profits for the last 4 years which were £10 335, £13 665, £16 902 and £17 538. The cost of the goodwill will be
A £58 440 **B** £29 220 **C** £34 440 **D** £14 610

15 The assets of a business that is being sold are valued at £76 200 and the liabilities at £19 620. The purchase price has been agreed at the net value of the business plus twice the average of the profits for the last three years, namely £6720, £7380 and £7950. What is the price to be paid for the business?
A £76 935 **B** £58 050 **C** £56 580 **D** £71 280

16 When a new partner is admitted into partnership he often has to pay the existing partners for his share of the goodwill. This payment is known as
A capital **B** drawings **C** a premium **D** a discount

17 When a new partner is unable to pay a premium in cash, a Goodwill Account may be raised to overcome this difficulty. The necessary entries to record this are
- **A** debit Goodwill Account, credit Existing Partners' Capital Accounts
- **B** debit Existing Partners' Current Accounts, credit Goodwill Account
- **C** debit Existing Partners' Capital Accounts, credit Goodwill Account
- **D** debit Goodwill Account, credit Existing Partners' Current Accounts

18 Which of the following statements is *incorrect*? Goodwill is
- **A** the amount that has been paid over and above the net value of a business being purchased
- **B** the amount paid to acquire the right to represent the purchaser of a business as the successor to the business and to enjoy every right attaching to the business, capable of transfer
- **C** the total amount paid for the business
- **D** an intangible asset to be shown in the Balance Sheet

19 A. Morgan, a wholesaler whose capital on 31 December 19— was £6000, decided to admit E. Evans into partnership as an equal partner provided that E. Evans pays £4000 in cash and on condition that the value of the goodwill be fixed at £2500 and credited to A. Morgan. Immediately upon the admission of the new partner, the Balance Sheet of the partnership will show Capital Account

A Morgan £6000 and Evans £4000
B Morgan £6250 and Evans £6250
C Morgan £8500 and Evans £4000
D Morgan £7250 and Evans £5250

20 When goodwill is shown in the Balance Sheet it

A must be adjusted each year to show its true value
B must always remain at that same figure
C may be written off over a number of years if profits are sufficient
D should never be written down but should be increased when profits increase

16
Incomplete records

1 The capital of a business at the beginning of the year was £64 000 and at the end £78 400. There were no drawings. What was the net profit assuming that no new capital had been introduced?
A The net profit cannot be calculated from the above information
B £14 400
C £16 000
D No profit but a loss of £14 400

2 The capital of a business on 1 April 19— was £173 000 and on 31 March 19–1 was £185 000 and the drawings for the year were £10 000. What was the net profit or loss for the year?
A £12 000 profit
B £22 000 profit
C £2000 loss
D Cannot be calculated from the above information

3 The total debtors at the start of a year was £13 484 and at the end £15 240. The total cash received from debtors was £192 880. What were the sales?
A £192 880 **B** £192 636 **C** £191 144 **D** £194 636

4 The total creditors at the beginning of the year was £9924 and at the end of the year £11 242. The total amount paid to the creditors during the period was £145 288. What were the total purchases for the period?
A £146 606 **B** £143 870 **C** £145 288 **D** £152 606

5 The capital of a business at the start of a year was £24 400 and at the end £28 300. The drawings for the year were £4500 and the total expenses £3650. What was the gross profit?
A £8400 **B** £3900 **C** £3050 **D** £12 050

6 The whole of a firm's stock was destroyed by fire. From the following information, what was the value of the stock lost?

Stock at start of year £6200. Purchases and sales to the date of the fire £140 000 and £185 300, respectively. The percentage gross profit to the cost of sales was $33\frac{1}{3}\%$.

The value of stock lost
A was £6200

B was £7225
C was £8400
D cannot be calculated from this information only

7 A trader is able to supply the following information:

	1 Jan 19—	31 Dec 19—
	£	£
Premises	15 000	15 000
Cash at bank	540	1 080
Stock	2 040	2 910
Debtors	1 410	1 680
Creditors	2 577	2 790

In addition he states he withdrew £2250 for his own use. His net profit for the year, ended 31 December 19—
A was £3717 profit
B was £1680 profit
C was −£810 (loss)
D cannot be calculated from the figures given

******

Consider the following information and then answer questions 8–12. Below is a summary of the Cash and Bank Accounts of a business for the year ended 31 December 19—

	£
Cash received from customers	240 000
Payments to suppliers	192 400
Personal drawings	10 000
General expenses	17 200
Wages	20 000

At 1 January 19— the financial position of the business was:

	£		£
Capital	31 360	Fixed assets	11 120
Creditors	10 800	Cash in hand and at bank	240
		Debtors	4 800
		Stock	26 000
	42 160		42 160

On 31 December 19— the amount owing to suppliers was £12 200, the total of debts outstanding amounted to £5200 and the stock in hand was £28 000.

8 The balance of cash in hand and at bank on 31 December 19— was
A £400 **B** £640 **C** £840 **D** £600

9 The total sales for the year were
A £240 000 **B** £360 400 **C** £240 400 **D** £144 400

10 The total purchases for the year were
A £193 800 **B** £192 400 **C** £181 600 **D** £191 000

11 The gross profit for the year was
A £47 600 **B** £49 600 **C** £48 600 **D** £49 000

12 The net profit for the year was
A £11 400 **B** £12 400 **C** £15 400 **D** £1400

13 The profit and loss of a business is calculated from the following information:

	1 Jan 19— £	31 Dec 19— £
Fixed assets	16 300	15 750
Stock	12 000	13 350
Debtors	6 750	7 900
Creditors	13 350	10 800
Balance at bank	8 500	9 600

The net profit will be
A £6800 **B** £5600 **C** £5100 **D** £4600

14 A Statement of Affairs is similar to a
A Balance Sheet
B Statement of Account
C Bank Statement
D Bank Reconciliation Statement

15 The total of debts outstanding at the beginning of the year was £2650 and at the end of the year £3375. During the year £32 640 was received from customers, allowing them £240 cash discount and £320 was written off as bad debts. The total sales will be
A £32 800 **B** £33 925 **C** £33 200 **D** £33 365

16 The total of the creditors at the beginning of the year was £4600 and at the end £5250. During the year £26 500 was paid to suppliers and £130 was received in cash discounts from these suppliers. From this information it would appear that the purchases for the year were
A £26 500 **B** £27 150 **C** £27 028 **D** £27 280

17 A fire destroyed part of the premises and some of the records of a company. The proprietor stated that he was able to obtain the following information:

	1 Jan 19— £	31 Dec 19— £
Cash balance	180	225
Debtors	6200	7550

Cash banked during the year £231 245

He also states that his only income is from sales all of which were banked after paying wages £200 per week and sundry expenses totalling £2560. In order to make a claim for loss of profits he needs to know the sales for the year. If it can be calculated from the above information, it will be

A £242 205
B £245 555
C £240 885
D it cannot be calculated due to insufficient information

18 The capital of a sole trader on 1 January 19— was £12 900 and on 31 December 19— £11 640. During the year his drawings were £6900 but his car was sold for £5000 and the proceeds put into the business together with a further £4000 which he obtained as a mortgage on the business premises. From these figures his net profit or loss will be

A loss £1260 **B** profit £3960 **C** profit £640 **D** loss £3360

19 A fire destroyed many of the records of a business. From the remaining records the following information was obtained:

1 Jan 19—	Total assets except for debtors £96 000, capital £5200, remaining liabilities £94 700
31 Dec 19—	Debtors £4600, receipts from customers during the year £26 300

Using this information the sales for the year will be

A £26 300 **B** £30 900 **C** £25 600 **D** £27 000

20 A fire destroyed many records of a business. From the remaining records the following information was obtained:

1 Jan 19—	Total assets £56 000, capital £6000 (the only other liabilities were trade creditors)
31 Dec 19—	Creditors £48 500. Amounts paid to suppliers during the year £151 200

Using this information the purchases should be

A £151 200 **B** £199 700 **C** £149 700 **D** £152 700

17
Easy questions on a variety of topics

Consider the following Balance Sheet and then answer questions 1–5.

Balance Sheet
(as at 31 December 19—)

			£
Capital			23 560
Represented by			
Fixed assets	*Cost*	*Depreciation*	*Book value*
	£	£	£
Premises	10 000		10 000
Machinery	4 000	400	3 600
	14 000	400	13 600
Current assets	£	£	
Stock		5 200	
Debtors	4 400		
Less Provision for bad debts	1 000	3 400	
Cash at bank		3 920	
Cash in hand		240	
		12 760	
Less Current liabilities			
Sundry creditors		2 800	
			9 960
			23 560

1 The total of fixed assets is
A £14 000 **B** £13 600 **C** £12 760 **D** £26 360

2 The total of current assets is
A £2800 **B** £13 600 **C** £12 760 **D** £9640

3 The working capital is
A £26 360 **B** £9640 **C** £9960 **D** £20 760

4 If $\frac{1}{4}$ of the stock is sold for £1400 then the total of the assets will be
A £26 360 **B** £23 560 **C** £25 160 **D** £26 460

5 If a supplier's account for £400 is paid less 5% cash discount then the total of the assets will be
A £26 360 **B** £25 980 **C** £25 960 **D** £26 560

6 To create a provision for discounts allowed it will be necessary to
- **A** debit Profit and Loss Account and credit Provision for Discounts Allowed Account
- **B** debit Provision for Discounts Allowed Account and credit Profit and Loss Account
- **C** debit Customers' Personal Accounts and credit Provision for Discounts Allowed Account
- **D** debit Discounts Allowed Account and credit Provision for Discounts Allowed Account

7 If the actual bad debts in any year are greater than the balance on the Provision for Bad Debts Account
- **A** it is only necessary to credit Profit and Loss Account with the difference
- **B** the total of the bad debts should be debited to the Profit and Loss Account together with any increase required in the provision
- **C** the total of the bad debts should be debited to Profit and Loss Account together with the difference between the bad debts and the provision for bad debts
- **D** it is only necessary to debit Profit and Loss Account with the difference

8 Which one of the following would appear as a current liability in the Balance Sheet?
- **A** Wages due
- **B** Rent receivable due
- **C** Insurance premiums paid in advance
- **D** Advertising charges carried forward

9 Which of the following transactions will affect the Capital Account of a business?
- **A** Goods for resale purchased on credit
- **B** A receipt from a debtor for £210
- **C** A sale of goods which cost £150 for £220
- **D** A purchase of a machine for use in the business

10 Discount columns in the Cash Book
- **A** need not be used if there is a Discount Account in the ledger
- **B** are only memoranda columns
- **C** are themselves Ledger Accounts
- **D** are only used when trade discount is given or received

11 The particulars of most of the transactions entered on the debit of the Bank Account in the Cash Book are obtained from
- **A** the bank paying-in book
- **B** bank statements
- **C** cheque stubs
- **D** debit notes

12 The particulars of transactions entered on the credit of the Bank Account in the Cash Book are usually obtained from
A the bank paying-in book **C** cheque stubs
B bank statements **D** credit notes

13 When Final Accounts are prepared, if a Provision for Bad Debts Account is maintained the balance on this account
A is written off to Profit and Loss Account
B stays as an open account and is only adjusted in following years
C is shown as an asset in the Balance Sheet
D is written off to Profit and Loss Account if there is sufficient profit

14 Which of the following is *not* a liability?
A Expenses due
B Rent received in advance
C Subscriptions received in respect of the following year
D Rates paid in advance

15 Shares on which a dividend cannot be paid in one year but which are entitled to any arrears out of future profits are known as
A ordinary shares
B deferred shares
C participating preference shares
D cumulative preference shares

16 The value of a trader's stock at cost on 1 January 19— was £9000. His records for the year ended 31 December 19— showed sales £99 000 and purchases £69 000. His percentage gross profit to sales was $33\frac{1}{3}$. What was the value of his stock on 31 December 19—?
A £12 000 **B** £7000 **C** £1000 **D** £10 000

17 A limited company can pay dividends
A only when there has been a profit for that year
B only when there has been a profit for that year or profits brought forward from previous years
C whenever the directors wish
D provided that the shareholders agree

18 Which of the following is *not* a convention of accounting?
A Consistency **B** Materiality **C** Conservatism **D** Moderation

19 The following information was obtained from the Final Accounts of G. Green:

Sales	£330 000
Opening stock	£ 9 000
Closing stock	£ 13 000
Purchases	£235 000

Using the above information G. Green's rate of stock turnover will be
A 42 times **B** 33 times **C** $11\frac{4}{11}$ times **D** 21 times

20 Which of the following is revenue expenditure for a garage proprietor? The purchase of
A a car for resale
B a van for use in the business
C tools for use in the workshop
D petrol pumps

21 Computer software packages favoured by accountants particularly when preparing final accounts are known as
A sort programs
B spread sheets
C merge programs
D database management systems (DBMS)

22 A computer programming language in which each statement in the source code is equal to one or at the most a few statements in machine language is known as
A a low-level language
B FORTRAN
C BASIC
D COBOL

23 Which of the following are aids to program designers?
A Flowcharts
B Structure charts
C Decision tables
D All three of the above

24 Which of the following statements is false?
A COM can store large volumes of data in a small space
B Recording on COM can be 25–50 times faster than printing
C Microfilm reproduces an exact facsimile
D COM equipment is cheaper than printers

25 Which of the following input devices is most suitable for processing bank cheques?
A OCR **B** MICR **C** Tape **D** Light pens

18

Harder questions on a variety of topics

Consider the following Trading and Profit and Loss Account and then answer questions 1–6.

Trading and Profit and Loss Account
(for year ended 31 December 19—)

		£	£	£
Sales			49 720	
Less Sales returns			520	
				49 200
Less Stock at start		12 000		
Plus Purchases	28 400			
Plus Carriage inwards	800			
	29 200			
Less Purchase returns	1 200			
		28 000		
		40 000		
Less Stock at end		20 000		20 000
Gross profit				29 200
Plus Discounts				120
				29 320
Less Expenses				
Rent		6 000		
Plus Rent accrued		1 200	7 200	
Carriage outwards			220	
Rates		6 400		
Less Rates prepaid		1 600	4 800	
Salaries			10 800	
Light and heat			1 200	
Discounts			180	
				24 400
Net profit				4 920

1 The cost of the goods sold is
A £20 000 **B** £36 000 **C** £49 200 **D** £37 200

2 The net profit as a percentage of sales is
A 10% **B** 33% **C** 15% **D** 20%

3 The returns outwards are
A £520 **B** £800 **C** £1200 **D** £680

4 The carriage on sales is
A £800 **B** £220 **C** £580 **D** £1200

5 Had there been a purchase of additional fixtures for £1200 then the net profit would have been
A £3720
B the same, ie £4920
C £6120
D either A or B depending upon whether the fixtures were new or second-hand

6 The amount of discount received is
A £120 **B** £180 **C** £60 **D** £300

7 The Sales Returns Day Book has been incorrectly totalled as £150 instead of £160. To correct this error it is necessary to
A debit Sales Returns Account £10
B credit Sales Returns Account £10
C debit Sales Returns Account £10 and credit the Personal Account £10
D debit the Personal Account £10 and credit Sales Returns Account £10

8 Which of these statements is *false*? After Final Accounts have been prepared
A wages due will appear as a credit balance on the Wages Account
B rates paid in advance will appear as a debit balance on the Rates Account
C rent received in advance will appear as a credit balance on the Rent Account
D insurance premiums paid in advance will appear as a credit balance on the Insurance Account

9 A voluntary appropriation of profits to strengthen the financial position of a business is known as a
A provision **C** payment in advance
B reserve **D** dividend

10 Which of these statements is *false*?
A A credit is a gain or a liability
B If there is no agreement then partners cannot share profits in the proportions of two thirds and one third
C A debit is a loss or an asset
D If the balance on the Cash and Bank Accounts increases then there must be a profit

11 Which is the correct statement?
- **A** A limited company cannot be insolvent as it always has a share capital to use to pay any debts
- **B** A sole proprietor of a business is insolvent when his capital appears on the liability side of the Balance Sheet
- **C** All sleeping partners must be limited partners
- **D** A partner may have to pay not only his share of any losses but also his partners' share of those losses

12 Which is the *incorrect* statement?
- **A** The wages of employees are charges against profits but wages of partners are appropriations of profits
- **B** Profit is affected by the basis chosen for the valuation of stock
- **C** Profit means an increase in the net value of assets
- **D** Interest on debentures and dividends on shares are charges against profits

******

The following Balance Sheet has been prepared without some of the sub-headings and details. Consider the Balance Sheet and then answer questions 13–16.

J. Summers: Balance Sheet
(as at 31 December 19—)

	£	£	£
Capital (Balance)		66 480	
Add Net profit		19 360	
		85 840	
Less Drawings		14 000	71 840
Represented by			
Freehold premises		35 200	
Plant and machinery	20 000		
Less Depreciation	2 000	18 000	
Vans	8 000		
Less Depreciation	1 600	6 400	59 600
Stock	8 480		
Debtors	18 560		
Cash at bank	4 800	31 840	
Creditors		19 600	12 240
			71 840

13 The amount £71 840 represents
- **A** working capital
- **B** total liabilities
- **C** net capital employed
- **D** nominal capital

14 The amount £59 600 is the value of the

A fixed assets
B working capital
C current assets
D net capital employed

15 The amount £12 240 is the value of the

A net capital employed
B working capital
C ownership equity
D current assets

16 The amount £31 840 is the value of the

A working capital
B current assets
C ownership equity
D net capital employed

17 Which is the correct statement?

A Discount can appear only on the debit side of the Profit and Loss Account
B The balance on the Provision for Bad Debts Account appears on the debit side of the Trial Balance
C Rates paid in advance appears as an asset in the Balance Sheet
D A Receipts and Payments Account is similar to a Profit and Loss Account

18 The current assets of a business are: debtors, stock, cash at bank, cash in hand. The correct order for these assets in the Balance Sheet is

A stock, cash at bank, cash in hand, debtors
B stock, debtors, cash in hand, cash at bank
C stock, debtors, cash at bank, cash in hand
D debtors, stock, cash in hand, cash at bank

19 Which of the following is *incorrect*?

A To head a Profit and Loss Account 'For period ended 31 December 19—'
B To head a Balance Sheet 'For period ended 31 December 19—'
C To head an Income and Expenditure Account 'For period ended 31 December 19—'
D All three of the above

20 A trader has made a profit during his trading year but his cash at the bank is now less than it was at the beginning of the year. This may be because

A he has bought additional premises
B his debtors have increased
C his creditors have decreased
D all of the above have taken place

21 Which of the following is a type of main memory?

A RAM
B ROM
C Both A and B above
D Neither A nor B above

22 Which of the following is *not* a high-level language?

A COBOL
B FORTRAN
C BASIC
D BINARY

23 A peripheral device in which the medium used is a magnetic disc is
A a disc drive
B an assembler
C a processor
D a compiler

24 A data processing technique used to show a sequence of events in a system including both computer and non computer activities is known as a
A page printer
B drum
C DASD (direct access storing device)
D flowchart

25 Which of the following output devices would be most suitable for a company which has to provide a very large number of statements in a short time?
A Teletypewriter
B Graphic display unit
C Laser printer
D VDU

19
Difficult questions on a variety of topics

1 The credit balance on a Suspense Account is £320. Upon further examination of the books it is found that a purchase on credit from D. Baker for £160 had been posted wrongly to the debit of C. Baker's Account. When this error is corrected the balance on the Suspense Account will be

A £480 credit **C** nil
B £120 credit **D** £320 credit

2 A company's Balance Sheet as at 31 March 19— showed

	£	£
Total of debts outstanding	5000	
less Provision for bad debts	250	4750

Particulars for the following years were

	31 March 19–1	31 March 19–2
	£	£
Debtors before deductions for provisions	4600	5800
Actual amount of bad debts written off	340	250

If the Provision for Bad Debts Account is to be maintained at 5% of the total of debts outstanding, the total amount for bad debts plus the provision for bad debts for both years will be

	19–1	19–2
A	£230	£290
B	£320	£230
C	£320	£310
D	£570	£540

3 A Trial Balance showed total of debts outstanding £3600, provision for bad debts £160 and provision for discounts allowed £80. It is required to maintain these provisions at 5% and $2\frac{1}{2}$%, respectively. The amount to be charged to Profit and Loss Account to include both provisions will be

A £300 **B** £25.50 **C** £5.50 **D** £230

4 The missing item in the following account is

Bad Debts and Provision for Bad Debts Account

19—			£		19—			£	
31 Dec	Customers Account		50	00	1 Jan	Balance	b/d	150	00
	Balance	c/d	200	00	31 Dec	?			
			250	00				250	00
					19–1	Provision balance	b/d	200	00

A balance £100
B Profit and Loss Account £100
C Customers Account £100
D Sales Account £100

5 A fire destroyed the stock and some of the records of a business. From the records available the following information was obtained:

Stock at start of period	£3800
Sales to date of fire	£155 000
Purchases to date of fire	£124 400

It was the policy of the firm to calculate its selling price at a mark up of 25% on invoice price. An insurance claim for the loss of stock based on these figures will be
A £4200 **B** £3700 **C** £4300
D impossible to calculate from these figures alone

******

Consider the following Balance Sheet and then answer questions 6–10.

H. Harris: Balance Sheet
(as at 1 January 19—)

	£		£
Capital	11 240	Fixed assets	11 200
Trade creditors	19 060	Stock	9 040
		Debtors	7 620
		Cash at bank	2 440
	30 300		30 300

Mr Harris stated that he pays all his takings into the bank and makes all payments by cheque.

The following information has been extracted from the records for the year ended 31 December 19—:

	£
Receipts from customers	173 000
Payments to suppliers	124 620
Private drawings	10 800
Sundry expenses	6 400
Wages	28 000

On 31 December 19— his debtors were £9270, his stock was valued at £10 400 and his creditors amounted to £20 400. Using the information above calculate the answers to the following questions.

6 The bank balance at 31 December 19— was
A £5620 **B** £3180 **C** £5420 **D** £10 420

7 The purchases for the year were
A £122 970 **B** £123 280 **C** £126 270 **D** £125 960

8 The sales for the year were
A £173 000 **B** £163 730 **C** £174 650 **D** £189 890

9 The net profit for the year was
A £50 050 **B** £15 650 **C** £4840 **D** £26 640

10 The gross profit for the year
A was £50 050
B was £48 690
C was £60 850
D cannot be calculated from the information given

11 The Receipts and Payments Account of a tennis club showed rent paid £1200. At the commencement of the year the club owed rent £200 and at the end of the year £300. The amount to be charged to Income and Expenditure Account for the year will be
A £1200 **B** £1300 **C** £1100 **D** £1600

12 The secretary of a hockey club informs you that at the beginning of the year there were subscriptions owing by members £160 and £60 paid in advance. At the end of the year subscriptions owing by members amounted to £140 while the total received for subscriptions during the year was £10 240. The amount to be shown in the Income and Expenditure Account for subscriptions for the year will be
A £10 240 **B** £10 360 **C** £10 000 **D** £10 280

13 An Income and Expenditure Account shows 'Rates £650'. At the commencement of the year the rates owing amounted to £150 while at the end of the year £75 rates were paid in advance. The amount to be shown in the Receipts and Payments Account for rates will be
A £875 **B** £650 **C** £425 **D** £575

14 After Final Accounts had been prepared it was noticed that a parcel of goods costing £200 had not been included in the value of the stock neither for this year nor the previous year's stocktake. To correct this error which of the following adjustments to the profit would be necessary?
A Increase both this year and last year by £200
B Increase last year only by £200

C Increase this year only by £200
D Make no adjustment as it would not affect the profit of either year

******

Consider the following Trading Account and then answer questions 15–17.

Trading Account
(for year ended 31 December 19—)

	£	£
Sales		178 776
Less Stock 1 Jan 19—	13 300	
Purchases	152 176	
	165 476	
less Stock 31 Dec 19—	14 204	
Cost of goods sold		151 272
Gross profit		27 504

15 The rate of turnover is
A 11 times **C** 12.6 times
B 13 times **D** 6.5 times

16 The percentage gross profit to sales is
A 6.5% **B** 15.38% **C** 18.18% **D** 13%

17 Assume the rate of turnover was 12 times and the sales, gross profit and purchases remain the same, the average stock
A will be £6302
B will be £12 606
C will be £25 208
D cannot be calculated from this information only

18 Amortisation is
A the same as depreciation but usually used for leases
B the same as discounts
C the same as obsolescence
D the paid up capital of a limited company

******

Consider the following information and then answer questions 19 and 20.

Draft Final Accounts had been prepared showing as an asset in the Balance Sheet 'Suspense Account £50'. Later the errors were found and the Suspense Account was balanced as follows:

Suspense Account

Difference in Trial Balance		50	00	R. Rose (debtor)		40	00
P. Thorn (debtor)		10	00	Purchases Account		20	00
		60	00			60	00

19 After making the above corrections the net profit will be
- **A** reduced by £20
- **B** reduced by £50
- **C** the same as before
- **D** increased by £20

20 After balancing the Suspense Account the other alterations in the Balance Sheet will be
- **A** Capital Account reduced by £50
- **B** Capital Account reduced by £20 and Debtors' Accounts increased by £30
- **C** Debtors' Accounts increased by £50
- **D** Capital Account increased by £20 and Debtors' Accounts increased by £70

SECTION 2

20

Questions on a variety of topics:

more than one correct answer may be possible

In this section there may be one, two or three correct answers to each question. You are required to select your answers using the following code.

Select A where answer 1 (only) is correct
Select B where answer 2 (only) is correct
Select C where answer 3 (only) is correct
Select D where answers 1 and 2 are correct
Select E where answers 1 and 3 are correct
Select F where answers 2 and 3 are correct
Select G where answers 1, 2 and 3 are correct

1 Which of the following should be debited to the Profit and Loss Appropriation Account of a partnership?
   1 Partners' salary
   2 Interest on partners' drawings
   3 Interest on partners' capital

2 Which of the following is *not* capital expenditure?
   1 The purchase of a van by a butcher
   2 The purchase of a van for resale by a motor trader
   3 The purchase of a car for hire by a car rental company

3 In order to increase working capital a proprietor of a business could
   1 pay some of the creditors
   2 arrange for some of the debtors to pay their debts
   3 mortgage the premises

4 Consider the following information and then work out how many of the following statements are correct. The accounts of a tennis club for the year ended 31 December 19— showed 'Subscription received during the year £10 050', but this included £450 subscription paid in advance for the year ended 31 December 19–1.

1 The Receipts and Payments Account should show subscription received £10 050
2 The Income and Expenditure Account should show subscription £9600
3 The Balance Sheet should show 'Subscriptions paid in advance £450' as an asset

5 Which of the following transactions should be entered first in the Journal Proper?
1 Those that cannot be entered in any other book of prime entry
2 Capital items purchased on credit
3 Raw materials purchased on credit

6 Which of the following accounts may be contained in the Cash Book?
1 Discount Account
2 Bank Account
3 Cash Account

7 Which of the following may be reasons for depreciation?
1 Wear and tear
2 Inflation
3 Passage of time

8 If a trader works on a $33\frac{1}{3}\%$ mark-up and his sales for a month are £56 000 then his gross profit for the month will be
1 £14 000
2 25% of sales
3 50% of the cost of sales

9 Which of the following statements are true? Depreciation is
1 a way of providing funds for the replacement of an asset
2 an expense to be charged to Profit and Loss Account
3 the permanent decrease in value of an asset through wear and tear

10 Which of the following items appear in a Trading Account?
1 Carriage on sales
2 Representatives' commission
3 Cost of goods sold

11 Consider the following information and then state which of the following values of stock could be correct.

If the rate of turnover is 12 and the cost of the goods sold is £120 240

	Stock at start	Stock at end
1	£9 010	£11 030
2	£10 160	£10 020
3	£8 420	£11 620

12 Which of the following items appearing in a Manufacturing Account are factory overheads?
1 Power
2 Carriage
3 Works manager's salary

13 A machine costing £7000 was depreciated by £700 in its first year. Which of the following methods of depreciation might have been used?
1 Straight-line
2 Diminishing balance
3 Revaluation

14 The Bank Statement of a business shows a credit balance £30, but the Cash Book a £45 debit. Which of the following items would appear in a statement reconciling these two accounts?
1 A cheque for £15 paid into bank, entered in the Cash Book but not on the Bank Statement
2 A cheque for £25 drawn and entered in the Cash Book but not yet presented for payment
3 A standing order for £30 in the statement but not in the Cash Book

15 The capital of a company registered with the Registrar of Companies is known as the
1 issued capital
2 authorised capital
3 registered capital

16 A trader purchased goods for £2000, subject to a 20% trade discount and a further 5% cash discount if paid within 7 days of date of invoice. The trader would actually pay
1 £1500 if paid within the stipulated 7 days
2 £1520 if paid within the stipulated 7 days
3 £1600 if paid after the stipulated 7 days

17 A debit note is used when
1 an amount stated on an invoice sent to a customer is too small
2 an amount stated on an invoice sent to a customer is too large
3 fixtures and fittings are sold on credit

18 Which of the following may be considered to be an advantage of using the imprest system for petty cash?
1 The money in the hands of the petty cashier is limited to the amount of the imprest
2 Any extravagance will be revealed by comparing the amounts refunded
3 Less petty cash will be required weekly

19 Which of the following would be reasons for creating a Provision for Bad Debts Account?
1 Bad debts can be recovered more easily
2 The total of debts outstanding can be shown in the Balance Sheet at a more realistic figure
3 Actual bad debts can be written off to Profit and Loss Account

20 Which of the following statements are correct?
1 20% gross profit on sales is equivalent to 25% gross profit on cost of sales
2 25% gross profit on sales is equivalent to $33\frac{1}{3}$% gross profit on purchases
3 $33\frac{1}{3}$% gross profit on sales is equivalent to 50% gross profit on cost of sales

21 Which of the following statements are *false*?
1 If there is a net profit then there must be an increase in the cash or bank balances
2 The more money an owner of a business draws out from that business for his own private use, the less will be the net profit
3 If sales increase then there must be an increase in gross profit

22 A tennis club runs a bar whose takings during the year amounted to £15 200. These takings will be shown as debits in
1 the Cash or Bank Accounts
2 the Income and Expenditure Account
3 the Receipts and Payments Account

23 Which of the following statements relating to a partnership are *false*?
1 Profits and losses must always be shared equally
2 Interest must be charged on all drawings
3 All partners must contribute equally to the capital

24 After the preparation of the Final Accounts, the owner of a business discovered that an invoice for £60 from a supplier had not been entered in the Purchases Day Book. In order to correct this omission it would be necessary to amend the Balance Sheet by
1 increasing the stock and creditors by £60
2 increasing the capital and stock by £60
3 increasing the creditors and decreasing the capital by £60

25 An entry in the Purchases Day Book 'W. Williams £20' had been posted to the debit of W. Williams Account. In order to balance the Trial Balance before this error is discovered it will be necessary to open a Suspense Account with a
1 £40 debit **2** £40 credit **3** £20 credit

26 Which of the following statements are correct? A Statement of Affairs
1 shows the profit or loss
2 is similar to a Balance Sheet
3 is prepared in order to calculate the capital of a business when the records are incomplete

27 The purchase of a printing machine by a printer should first be entered in the
1 Purchases Day Book
2 Journal Proper if it were purchased on credit
3 Cash Book if it were purchased and paid for by cash

28 A business selling office furniture purchases a desk on credit from Office Supplies Ltd. The entries necessary to record this transaction will be

1 debit Purchases Account and credit Office Supplies Ltd Account if the desk was purchased for resale

2 debit Office Supplies Ltd Account and credit Purchases Account if the desk was purchased for resale

3 debit Office Furniture Account and credit Office Supplies Ltd Account if the desk was purchased for use in the office

29 Which of the following are fixed costs?

1 Depreciation (if calculated using the straight-line method)

2 Depreciation (if calculated on the number of hours worked)

3 Rent of factory

30 Which of the following are variable costs?

1 Rates

2 Power

3 Insurance of buildings

31 The owner of a business produces the following information concerning the rates of his premises:

Demands for half year ended		Date paid	
	£		
31 March 19–1	2350	15 October	19—
30 September 19–1	2460	20 April	19–1
31 March 19–2	2460	10 November	19–1

Consider the above information and then state which of the following amounts should appear as rates in his Profit and Loss Account for the year ended 31 December 19–1

1 £4865 **2** £4810 **3** £4920

32 Using the information in question 31 above, 'Rates paid in advance £1230' should appear as a

1 Current Asset in the Balance Sheet as at 31 December 19–1

2 Current Asset in the Balance Sheet as at 31 December 19—

3 debit balance on the Rates Account at 31 December 19–1

33 Consider the following Loan Interest Account and then state which of the following statements are correct

Loan Interest Account

19—			£	19—			£
31 Mar	Cash		320 00	1 Jan	Balance	b/d	160 00
30 Sep	Cash		300 00				
31 Dec	Balance	c/d	150 00	31 Dec	?		610 00
			770 00				770 00
				19–1			
				1 Jan	Balance	b/d	150 00

In the Final Accounts for the year ended 31 December 19—

1 loan interest £770 will appear in the Profit and Loss Account
2 loan interest £610 will appear in the Profit and Loss Account
3 the balance £150 will appear as a current liability in the Balance Sheet

34 A debenture is

1 the same as a preference share
2 a long-term liability
3 an acknowledgement of a debt by a limited company

35 In a partnership, if the partners wish to pay themselves wages for working in the business, then they may do so provided

1 the partnership agreement does not specifically forbid the payment of such wages
2 there is a profit
3 the partnership agreement allows the payment of wages or salaries to partners

Answers

Section One

Question Number	Chapter 1	2	3	4	5	6	7	8	9	10	11	12	13	14	15	16	17	18	19	Question Number
1	C	A	A	C	C	D	D	A	C	B	B	B	B	D	C	B	B	A	C	1
2	A	B	B	D	C	C	B	D	A	D	A	C	D	B	C	B	C	A	C	2
3	B	A	B	B	C	B	C	B	B	D	C	D	C	B	D	D	C	C	B	3
4	A	C	B	D	B	D	A	C	D	A	D	D	D	A	A	A	D	B	B	4
5	C	D	A	C	C	D	D	B	D	C	B	A	B	C	B	D	B	B	A	5
6	A	C	D	B	C	A	A	A	B	C	D	D	D	C	C	B	A	A	A	6
7	B	C	C	C	C	D	B	B	C	C	C	A	C	B	D	A	B	A	D	7
8	C	B	D	D	A	B	A	D	B	D	A	C	C	C	C	B	A	D	C	8
9	C	C	A	D	B	C	B	C	D	B	B	B	D	D	A	C	C	B	B	9
10	B	A	C	B	C	B	C	D	C	A	D	C	D	D	C	A	B	D	A	10
11	A	C	B	C	D	C	A	D	D	C	B	A	D	D	B	C	A	D	B	11
12	B	C	B	A	A	A	A	A	B	A	D	B	D	C	B	A	C	D	D	12
13	D	C	C	B	D	A	C	C	C	D	C	D	B	B	D	B	B	C	A	13
14	B	B	A	C	B	A	C	D	B	B	D	D	D	D	B	A	D	A	B	14
15	A	B	A	B	C	C	B	D	A	B	A	D	A	D	D	B	D	B	A	15
16	D	D	A	C	D	A	D	B	C	A	A	A	A	A	C	D	A	B	B	16
17	C	B	D	A	C	C	C	B	B	D	B	C	B	A	A	B	B	C	B	17
18	A	B	B	D	B	D	B	A	A	B	A	B	A	B	C	D	D	C	A	18
19	A	A	B	C	B	D	D	A	C	C	D	C	B	C	C	D	D	D	A	19
20	A	B	C	A	C	D	C	B	B	B	A	A	C	A	C	C	A	D	B	20
21																	B	C		21
22																	A	D		22
23																	D	A		23
24																	D	D		24
25																	B	C		25

Section Two

Question Number	Answer	Question Number	Answer
1	E	19	B
2	B	20	E
3	C	21	G
4	D	22	E
5	D	23	G
6	F	24	C
7	E	25	B
8	D	26	F
9	F	27	F
10	C	28	E
11	E	29	E
12	E	30	B
13	G	31	A
14	A	32	E
15	F	33	F
16	F	34	F
17	A	35	C
18	D		